Green S Cookbook

Famous Nova Scotia Recipes
from the Kitchen of Hilda Zinck

Nimbus Publishing Limited
P.O. Box 9301, Station A
Halifax, Nova Scotia
B3K 5N5

Design: Paul MacCormick

Printed and Bound in Canada by Gagne Printing

Canadian Cataloguing in Publication Data

Zinck, Hilda M., 1906—

Green Shutters Cookbook

Includes index.
Reprint. Previously published: Tantallon, N.S. Four East, 1982.

ISBN 0-921054-57-2

1. Cookery—I. Title
TX714.Z56 1991 641.5 C91-097599-X

To
My Mother
Mrs. Daniel E. Grimm

A Brief Historical Sketch of Green Shutters

The photograph of the old "GREEN SHUTTERS INN" which appears on the title page of this book was once a popular tourist home, which stood at Mader's Cove, on Nova Scotia's south shore.

The 117 year old landmark, which overlooked Mahone Bay harbor, was purchased by a seafaring gentleman, named Peter Strum, in 1812. During this historical era, American privateers hovered off the Nova Scotian coast and were a constant threat to adventurous seamen such as Peter Strum and his father. Finally realizing "life and limb" to be more important than constant danger, they decided to give up their frolicking sea adventures and endeavor to make a living on this 60-acre grant, where life would be safer, although decidedly less exciting for them.

The original building was destroyed by fire in 1855, and was immediately replaced by a duplex-style structure, later to be occupied by Peter's two sons, Alfred and Charles Strum.

The granddaughter, Miss Laura J. Strum, had the home remodelled in 1932, later opening it to the public as a comfortable and attractive travellers inn. The old Dutch Ovens, the cozy fireplaces, the wide pine floor boards, and the valuable antique pieces, made it a most appropriate setting for this enterprise.

During the War years 1942-1944 Miss Strum opened her home to *Ajax Hospitality Headquarters* registered as a War Charity in Halifax. She received honorable mention for her services in catering to, and entertaining survivors of the torpedoed ships of the Royal Navy including servicemen from England, Scotland and Wales.

The Inn and tourist business was successfully carried on by Hilda M. Zinck from 1951 to 1963, during which time many prominent guests stayed over at the Inn and enjoyed Mrs. Zinck's warm hospitality. It was at this time the cookbook, **Green Shutters Cookbook** was conceived and later published by Mrs. Zinck. Mrs. Zinck sold **Green Shutters** in 1964 to take over the management of one of the most distinguished Halifax city clubs. The new owners, Mr. and Mrs. Eric Miller, subsequently decided that the Green Shutters building was structurally unsound for preservation, whereupon this impressive landmark was demolished in 1972.

Before You Begin . . .

For perfect results follow, carefully, instructions for baking and cooking.

Have all necessary utensils and ingredients ready before starting work.

Read, carefully, all recipes before beginning to combine ingredients.

For satisfactory results accurate measurements are essential in cooking. Have an 8-oz measuring cup with suitable divisions marked; standard size teaspoons and tablespoons. All measurements given are level.

For liquid measurements, fill cup to the 1 cup mark.

For dry ingredients, fill measuring cup or spoon and level with a knife. When half a spoonful is required, fill spoon and then divide lengthwise of the spoon and scrape out one-half. When one-quarter of a spoonful is required, divide crosswise the other half.

For shortening, pack and level the measuring cup or spoon and level with a knife. Always select a good grade of shortening.

Unless otherwise specified, all flour used in these recipes is All-Purpose. When All-Purpose flour is substituted for Pastry flour, it is a good rule to use two tablespoons less flour to each cup. Sift flour once before measuring. After measuring, flour should be sifted several times to give cake a better texture.

All leavening powders, whether baking powder, soda or cream of tartar, should be mixed and sifted with the flour several times before being added to the batter.

Ground spices, such as ginger, cinnamon, cloves etc., should be mixed and sifted with the flour and then added to the batter.

Cocoa may be used to replace chocolate in cake making, by substituting one-third cup of cocoa and two teaspoonfuls shortening for every ounce (or square) of chocolate designated in the recipe.

When combining eggs and a hot mixture always add the hot mixture to the eggs — not the eggs to the hot mixture.

Great care should be taken in combining ingredients, and in the baking. If oven temperature is not satisfactory the cake may be a failure, despite the most careful preparation.

Serve hot food hot from hot dishes. Serve cold food chilled from chilled dishes.

In making soups, chowders, and stews the exact amount of salt cannot be given. Use enough to bring out the true flavor.

Do not be an "oven-peeper" as peeping results in a loss of heat and causes baking failure.

Abbreviations and Measurements

tsp.	=	teaspoon
tsps.	=	teaspoons
tbsp.	=	tablespoon
tbsps.	=	tablespoons
oz.	=	ounce or ounces
lb.	=	pound
lbs.	=	pounds
pt.	=	pint
pts.	=	pints
qt.	=	quart
qts.	=	quarts
sq.	=	square or squares

dash or pinch	=	less than $\frac{1}{8}$ teaspoon
1 pint	=	2 cups
1 quart	=	4 cups
1 tbsp.	=	3 teaspoons
$\frac{1}{4}$ cup	=	4 tablespoons

All units of measure given in this book are based on standard measurements commonly used in Canada.

Oven Temperatures

Slow oven .... 275 to 325 degrees 149c
Moderate oven .... 325 to 375 degrees 177c
Moderately Hot oven .... 375 to 400 degrees 190c
Hot oven .... 400 to 450 degrees 205c
Very Hot oven .... 450 to 475 degrees 232c

Metric Conversion Chart

Cooking Equivalents

1 tbsp. cornstarch = 14 grams
1 tbsp. coffee = 6 grams
1 tbsp. chopped onion = 10 grams
1 tbsp. butter = 14 grams
1 cup butter = 226 grams
1 cup granulated sugar = 226 grams
1 cup all-purpose flour = 113 grams
1 cup cake flour = 95 grams
1 cup breadcrumbs = 47 grams
1 cup rice = 226 grams
1 cup grated cheese = 113 grams

Cooking Measures

1 teaspoon = 5 milliliters
1 tablespoon = 15 milliliters
1 fluid ounce = 30 milliliters
¼ cup = 60 milliliters
⅓ cup = 80 milliliters
½ cup = 120 milliliters
⅔ cup = 160 milliliters
¾ cup = 180 milliliters
1 cup = 240 milliliters

Cooking Terms

Dredge — to apply a coat of any dry substance, such as flour, egg, crumbs, to the outside of the meat or fish.

Marinate — to allow the meat to stand in a mixture before cooking. The marinade varies and usually consists of oil, vinegar, lemon juice, wine, herbs or any other seasoning.

Pan-Broil — to cook, uncovered, in a hot skillet without fat. You pour off the fat from the meat as it cooks out.

Fry — to cook or saute in a skillet using a small amount of fat.

Deep-Fry — Using a deep skillet and sufficient fat or oil so that the food will float while frying.

Parboil — to partially cook food in boiling water before you cook it, according to the recipe.

Score — to make slits in the surface of the meat or pastry with a knife or scissors, usually preparatory to inserting seasonings.

Heeling — is the final basting of roast or any kind of meat and is often done using wine or brandy.

Helpful Hints

Bread for rolled sandwiches will roll better if first rolled lightly with a rolling pin.

Scissors dipped in hot water are convenient for cutting dried fruits and marshmallows.

Add a little softened bread or bread crumbs to hamburger steak to make it tender.

A teaspoonful of vinegar added to lard or shortening for frying prevents food from absorbing too much fat.

Garlic powder in now available and eliminates the trouble of grating the cloves, and the smell on fingers. A touch of it adds materially to salads and egg sandwiches.

A few sprigs of parsley dipped in vinegar or salt and eaten after a meal will prevent any breath odors of garlic or onion.

Eggs poached in milk are tastier and much more nutritious.

To keep cheese soft, wrap it in a piece of muslin or cloth which has been dipped in vinegar. Keep in a cold dry place.

Chicken livers are greatly improved in flavor, if soaked for a while in milk, before frying.

Short lengths of macaroni put into cake frosting make excellent holders. Sweet peas, pansies or other small flowers may be put into these "tubes." Put several holders in center of cake.

To cut hard butter, cover the blade of knife with wax paper or use knife heated in hot water.

To deter mold in bread tin, wash out bread tin with a mixture of two tablespoonsfuls vinegar to one quart of water.

Dried parsley retains its color and has many uses for flavoring soups, stews, White Sauce, mashed potatoes, etc.

All green vegetables should be cooked, uncovered, to preserve the color.

All vegetables should be thoroughly drained as soon as cooked and the water kept for stock.

Dry mustard mixed with lemon juice is excellent for over freshly boiled lobster.

The secret of a good curry is the long frying of curry powder.

To get the most juice from a lemon, roll it well before squeezing, or, put it into hot water for a few minutes. The latter method is excellent for freshening old lemons. Leave lemons in hot water for two hours or longer. To keep a cut lemon for a week or longer, store in plastic bag in refrigerator.

To make your icing sparkling white, mix the icing sugar with the juice from a lemon.

To keep egg whites from falling, add a pinch of cream of tartar when beating.

Onion juice added after a mixture is cooked gives a much better flavor than if the onion is cooked with the mixture. Grate onion to extract the juice.

One tablespoon cornstarch is equivalent in thickening to one egg.

To make colored sugar, add a few drops of food coloring to fine granulated sugar and work in with finger tips. Repeat until desired color is obtained.

Salt Shaker Tips: For batters or dough: 1 tsp. to 4 cups water
Cereals: 1 tsp. to 2 cups liquid
Soups and Sauces: 1 tsp. to 1 quart sauce or stock
Meat: 1 tsp. to 1 lb. meat
Vegetables: ½ tsp. to 1 lb. raw vegetables

1.   Main dishes

Fish

Listen, little fish, and a tale I'll relate,
So make yourself comfortable now on my plate.
This tale is true, so take heed, my dear,
If you had kept your mouth closed, you wouldn't
be here.

Steamed Clams

Clams for steaming should be bought in shells while still alive.
Wash well, changing water several times. Put into large pot or
steamer and add a little boiling water, allowing about ½ cup water
to 4 quarts of clams. Cover and steam until shells are partially open.
Serve clams in individual dishes. Best eaten with melted butter and
lemon juice.

Note: Reserve broth in which clams have been steamed. Strain and
serve in glasses.

Steamed Clams for a Party

Wash clams well. Put in kettle and add a small quantity of water
and 2 tbsps. lemon juice. Cover kettle and steam the clams only until
shells begin to open, about 10 minutes. Remove meat from shells
and wash lightly to remove sand. Drain well. Put in pan with butter,
chopped onions, a sprinkle of garlic and tarragon powder, salt and
pepper to taste, chopped parsley and 2 tbsps. dry white wine. Saute
all ingredients together. In the meantime clean shells of sand and set
up for filling. Fill shells with sauted mixture. Sprinkle with melted
butter and chopped parsley. Serve very hot.

Fried Clams

Clean fresh clams or use canned clams. Dry well. Dip each clam in beaten egg, then in fine bread crumbs. Fry in deep fat, heated to 375 degrees, for 1 minute. Drain on absorbent paper and serve at once. If preferred, clams may be sauted in butter.

Clam Bouillon

Put liquid in which clams have been steamed through a very fine strainer. Heat, season with salt, pepper, and a lump of butter. Serve very hot in bouillon cups. Add a spoonful of whipped cream, if desired.

Clams on Toast

Heat 1 can of clams, reserving a little of the cold liquor. Thicken heated clams with a little flour stirred into cold liquor. Pour over toast and serve hot.

Clam Fritters

2 dozen clams
2 cups flour
1 tsp. baking powder
½ tsp. salt

1 cup milk
½ cup clam liquor
2 eggs, beaten
⅛ tsp. pepper

Make a batter of the flour, baking powder, salt, pepper, milk, clam liquor and well beaten eggs. Chop the clams coarsely, add to the batter and drop by tablespoonfuls in deep fat heated to 375 degrees. Turn frequently until browned on all sides. Drain on absorbent paper. Sufficient for 6 servings.

Digby Clam Dip

1 4 oz. package cream cheese
2 tsps. lemon juice
4 tsps. clam juice
⅛ tsp. Tabasco sauce

½ cup clams, drained and finely chopped
Pinch of salt, pepper, and garlic

Have cheese at room temperature for one hour or longer. Cream cheese and combine with remaining ingredients. Chill. Save extra clam juice to thin dip as it thickens on standing.

Fried Oysters

Place oysters in cold salted milk for five minutes. Drain and roll in fine bread crumbs. Fry in butter or cooking oil; season. Or, roll oysters in salted flour, dip in slightly beaten egg and roll in fine dry bread crumbs. Fry in butter until a golden brown.

Note: Oysters will be light and puffy if a little baking powder is added to the flour in which oysters are rolled. For added flavor, add a little celery salt to the bread or cracker crumbs used in frying oysters.

Oven Fried Oysters

2 doz. oysters	2 tbsps. fat or cooking oil
1 tsp. salt	1 cup milk
Flour	½ cup fine dry bread crumbs

Dissolve salt in the milk. Dip oysters in a little flour, then in the salted milk, and cover with the crumbs. Place the coated oysters on a baking sheet, about one inch apart, and sprinkle with butter or oil. Cook in oven 500 degrees until browned.

Oyster Stew

3½ cups milk	⅛ tsp. pepper
2 tbsps. butter	1 pint oysters with liquor
1 tsp. salt	2 tbsps. butter

Scald the first four ingredients in double boiler. Heat oysters in liquor and butter, until the edges curl. Add to the heated milk and, if necessary, add more seasoning. Serve very hot. A dash of paprika may be sprinkled on top. If a thicker stew is desired, add a little flour, about 1½ tbsps. to ½ cup milk and thicken the milk mixture before adding oysters.

Fried Smelts

Clean smelts, remove heads and tails, and wipe clean with a damp cloth. Roll in flour or corn meal. Fry both sides in a little fat, until golden brown. Season to taste with salt and pepper.

Fried Scallops

Wipe scallops with a damp cloth. Fry in butter until a golden brown. Turn and brown on other side, seasoning both sides with salt and pepper.

French Fried Scallops

Wipe scallops with a damp cloth. Roll in flour to which has been added a pinch of baking powder; season with salt and pepper, dip in slightly beaten egg, and roll in dry bread crumbs. Fry in hot fat 3-4 minutes, or until golden brown.

Baked Scallops

Slice scallops horizontally and salt to taste. Cover with milk and simmer in a pan until cooked. Line a casserole with sliced buttered bread and cover with the scallops and milk. Cover lightly with crumbs and sprinkle with melted butter. Put pan under the broiler until crumbs are lightly browned, and serve at once.

Scallops on Half-Shell

Select large fresh scallops, allowing five to each serving. Season with salt and pepper and coat with powder-dry cracker crumbs. Put a small amount of butter in each shell. Arrange coated scallops and over this put 1 tbsp. dry sec sherry. Cook under grill for about 20 minutes.

Pan Fried or Broiled Halibut

Wipe fish dry. Cut in individual servings. Dip in fine cracker or cornflake crumbs until thoroughly coated. Season with salt and pepper. Fry in preheated pan (with as little fat as possible) until a golden brown. Turn with spatula, season the other side, and put pan into hot oven for about 12 minutes, or finish frying on top of stove. Serve with lemon wedges.

To broil, place coated pieces in a greased shallow pan; season, dot with butter and broil in a moderately hot broiler until brown. Turn, season and brown on the other side.

Note: Fish is done when it easily leaves the bone.

Baked Stuffed Haddock or Halibut

Clean a medium-sized haddock or halibut. Season with salt and stuff with the following:

2 cups soft bread crumbs	¼ cup melted butter
1 tsp. salt	¼ cut hot water
⅛ tsp. pepper	Marjoram or seasoning to taste
1 small onion, minced	

Bake in hot oven for 1 hour. Serve with butter, or White Sauce and garnish with parsley and lemon wedges.

Soused Herring or Mackerel

Clean fish and cut in serving pieces. Place in baking dish and cover with vinegar to which has been added a little sugar, salt, pepper and about 1 teaspoon whole spice. Bake in oven until tender, about 35 minutes. Serve hot or cold with baked potatoes.

Creamed Finnan Haddie

Cover finnan haddie with cold water; let come to the boiling point and simmer for a few minutes, using top of stove or oven. Drain fish. Put small pieces of butter over the top, dust lightly with flour and pour over it a little milk. Return to oven for about 15 minutes and just before ready to serve add about ½ cup sweet cream. Serve hot.

Boiled Lunenburg Lobster

Put live lobsters in large kettle of boiling, salted water, using about 2 tbsps. salt to a gallon of water. Boil for 15 to 25 minutes, depending on the size, or until they turn a bright red. With a sharp knife cut through the body, shell side up, to the end of tail. Crack claws. Serve hot on platter with small dish of drawn butter, lemon wedges. French Fried potatoes, and crisp green salad.

Note: Provide your guests with a sizeable bib for the pleasurable meal of this succulent denizen of the deep.

Broiled Lobster

For choice eating select lobster from 1½ and 2 lbs. Hold firmly large claws of live lobster while with a sharp knife you make a deep incision in body, beginning from head to end of tail. Discard the head sac, intestinal vein, and the spongy lungs. Remove and put into bowl the green tomalley, liver and coral. Mix with 1 cup bread or cracker crumbs, 1 tbsp. lemon juice, dash of salt and cayenne pepper, garlic salt, according to taste. Fill cavities of lobster with above mixture. Put on grill or bake in 375 degree oven for 30 to 40 minutes, depending on the size of lobster. Baste several times with melted butter and a little sherry before removing from oven. Serve piping hot.

Lobster Newburg

6 tbsps. butter
2 tbsps. flour
3 cups cut lobster
2 cups cream

3 egg yolks
1 tsp. sherry
3 tbsps. sherry or brandy
Dash paprika

Melt butter in top of double boiler. Stir in flour, add lobster, then seasoning and sherry. Beat egg yolks slightly and add cream. Mix well. Stir slowly into lobster. Cook slowly, stirring to thicken.

Lobster Thermidor

2 large boiled lobsters
3 tbsps. butter
3 tbsps. flour
1½ cups milk
¼ lb. fresh or 3-oz. can
  mushrooms

Dash paprika
⅛ tsp. dry mustard
¼ cup sherry
4 tbsps. grated cheese (optional)

Cut lobsters in half, lengthwise. Remove all meat and cut in small pieces. Melt butter and stir in flour. Add milk gradually and cook until sauce is smooth and thick. Fry mushrooms in a little butter, for a few minutes, or if canned ones are used, drain off liquid. Mix lobster meat, mushrooms, mustard, paprika and sherry with the white sauce. The addition of some chopped parsley is nice. Fill lobster shells with mixture, sprinkle with cheese and broil until cheese browns slightly.

Stuffed Fish Fillets

Arrange fillets of halibut, haddock or any white fish in large well greased muffin cups. Fill with a savory bread stuffing and bake in a hot oven 400 degrees for 25 minutes. Nice served with crisp rolls and tossed salad.

Fish Nests

Line large muffin tins with hot mashed potatoes, seasoned with salt and minced parsley. Make a big hollow in the center. Fill with any creamed fish, sprinkle with crumbs and dot with butter. Bake until crumbs are nicely browned. Serve hot.

Seafood Casserole

1 lb. fresh haddock fillet	1 14-oz. can frozen lobster meat
1 lb. fresh halibut	1 large onion
1½ lbs. scallops	4 cups well seasoned cream sauce
1 lb. shrimp	½ cup dry sherry (optional)

Poach haddock and halibut in as little water as possible, saving some of the stock for making cream sauce. Cut scallops in half or quarter them, according to size. Do not precook scallops and shrimp. Break up haddock and halibut in small pieces and place all the fish and chopped onion in large casserole. Pour cream sauce over fish and bake in oven 375° for about ½ hour. Decorate top of casserole with the lobster claws or strips of green pepper, if preferred.

Cream Sauce: 2 tbsps. butter, 2 tbsps. flour, ¼ tsp. salt, ⅛ tsp. pepper, 1 cup milk or ½ cup milk and ½ cup fish stock. Melt butter in heavy saucepan over low heat. Blend in seasonings and cook over low heat until mixture is smooth. Remove from heat and stir in milk. Bring to a boil and cook for 1 minute, stirring constantly.

Scallop Casserole

1 cup cooked rice	1 bag or equivalent of frozen
1 lb. scallops, uncooked	mixed vegetables
1 large onion, sautéd lightly	1 can mushroom soup
in butter	¼ cup milk mixed with the soup
1 green pepper, sautéd lightly	
in butter	

Put ingredients in casserole in layers or mix altogether. Sprinkle with bread crumbs and dot with butter. Bake, uncovered, at 350 degrees for about 40 minutes.

Tuna Casserole with Cucumbers

1 cup diced, unpared
    cucumbers
¼ cup sliced onion
¼ cup butter
¼ cup flour
2 cups milk
1½ tsp. monosodium glutamate
1 small bay leaf

¼ tsp. Tabasco sauce
1 tbsp. salt
3 quarts boiling water
2 cups shell macaroni
2 7 oz. cans tuna, drained
2 tbsps. chopped pimiento
1 cup sour cream
Buttered crumbs

In saucepan, saute cucumber and onion in butter until crisp tender (about 2 minutes). Remove with slotted spoon, making sure not to take up any of the butter. In same saucepan, quickly stir flour into butter. Gradually stir in milk; add 1½ tsps. salt, monosodium glutamate, Tobasco sauce and bay leaf. Cook, stirring constantly, until sauce boils for 1 minute. Remove from heat; discard bay leaf. Stir in cucumber and onion. Meanwhile, add 1 tablespoon salt to rapidly boiling water. Gradually add macaroni so that water continues to boil. Cook uncovered, stirring occasionally, until tender. Drain in collander. Mix together macaroni, cucumber sauce, tuna, pimiento and sour cream. Turn into 2-quart casserole; sprinkle with crumbs. Bake in 375 degree oven 20 minutes or until bubbling hot. Four to 6 servings.

Dutch Mess

1 lb. salt cod
6 large potatoes
2 or more large onions

1 cup diced salt pork
1 cup cream
Pepper to taste

Break up codfish in strips and soak in cold water for several hours. If too salty, change water and let soak a little longer. Pare the potatoes and cut in bite size pieces. Put potatoes and fish into pot and cook until potatoes are done. Drain well. Fry pork and onions until a golden brown; add cream and combine. Pour this over the fish and potatoes. Serve hot with applesauce, fried apples or any favorite relish. (Any leftover from this dish may be mashed and with the addition of a beaten egg and some finely minced parsley, made into fish cakes).

Fried Fish Cheeks

Select small-sized cheeks, if possible. Wash quickly and dry well with a damp cloth. Roll in finely crushed cornflakes or corn meal. Season, and brown on one side until a golden brown. Turn, season, and put into hot oven 375 degrees to complete cooking, about 15-20 minutes, according to thickness. Or, after seasoning and browning on both sides, complete cooking on top of stove, using as little fat as possible for frying.

Solomon Gundy

6 salt herring
3 large onions

½ cup sugar
Whole pickling spice

Soak herring in cold water overnight. Clean and remove skin; fillet, and cut in pieces. Arrange alternate layers of herring and onion slices. Heat, to boiling point, just enough vinegar to cover. Add sugar and spice and let simmer on back of stove until spice has flavored the vinegar. Cool; strain and pour over the herring and onions. Keep in cold place. Good to eat after several days.

There is a mistaken idea, by some people, that Solomon Gundy is raw fish. The vinegar tenderizes and preserves it, making it edible, very delicious and an excellent appetizer.

Salmon Scallop

1 lb. salmon, fresh or canned
3 cups buttered bread crumbs
2 hard cooked eggs, sliced

2 cups milk
2 tbsps. butter
2 tbsps. flour

Make a cream sauce with the butter, flour and milk. Add eggs and salmon. Place half the bread crumbs in casserole. Pour in the salmon mixture and put the remaining crumbs on top. Dot with butter and bake in oven 350 degrees until done.

Salmon Puff

2 cups flaked salmon	1 tbsp. lemon juice
3 cups mashed potatoes	1 tbsp. chopped celery or parsley
1 onion, finely minced	2 eggs, separated
1 tbsp. melted butter	

Mix the flaked fish and potatoes. Add all ingredients except the egg whites. Fold in the beaten whites lastly, place in a buttered casserole, dot with butter and bake in oven 350 degrees until nicely browned.

Eels

In pioneering times, for people living near the salt water, eels were a very important item of food. A woman was considered not ready for marriage until she could skin an eel, make a loaf of bread, and make all her husband's shirts.

Fried Eels: Clean eels, cut in about 3-inch size pieces and parboil in salted water for 8 minutes. Pour off water, and spread pieces on wire rack to drain well. Sprinkle both sides with salt and pepper. Dip each piece in melted butter, then in flour or corn meal, and fry in pork fat until nicely browned on both sides.

Seafood Cocktail

Line chilled cocktail or sherbet glass with crisp lettuce. Fill with cut up lobster, shrimp or mixed seafood and cover with the following sauce:

Shrimp Cocktail Sauce:

½ cup tomato ketchup	1 tbsp. grated horseradish
½ cup chili sauce	1 tbsp. finely minced celery
2 tbsps. white vinegar	1 tbsp. grated onion
1 tsp. Worcestershire sauce	1 tsp. salt

Combine ingredients. Blend well and keep refrigerated, stirring well before using. Add extra horseradish for a hotter sauce.

Lobster or Mixed Seafood Sauce:

1 cup Miracle Whip	1½ tsps. Tabasco sauce
½ cup tomato ketchup	Juice of ½ lemon

Lobster Cream Dip for Chips

| 4 oz. cream cheese | 1 tbsp. sour cream or brandy |
| 1 can lobster paste | Finely minced lobster, if desired |

Mix all ingredients. Blend thoroughly and refrigerate until ready to serve.

Fish in Batter

Select firm, fresh fish, preferably haddock (if frozen fish is used it must be thawed and well dried). Cut fish in 2 inch squares. Dip each piece in batter, until completely coated, and fry in deep fat, pre-heated to 375 degrees, until a golden brown. Serve with tomato or chili sauce.

Batter:

1 cup all-purpose flour	2 eggs, beaten
1 tsp. baking powder	⅔ cup milk
1 tsp. salt	1 tbsp. melted butter

Combine eggs, milk and butter; add to dry ingredients, stirring until well blended.

Note: This batter may also be used for coating chicken for deep frying.

The best way to cook halibut, haddock, or salmon is by placing the fish in cookery parchment or aluminum foil; season with salt, tie securely, and place in a moderate amount of boiling water. By this method of cooking, the juices are retained and may be used in the making of a sauce for fish.

Meat

It is so distrubing, and really has us beat,
When we are like this, we are called dressed meat.

Roast Beef

Always select top quality beef. The best cuts are Prime Rib, Blade Roast, Sirloin Tip and T-Bone.

Put roast into pan, fat side up. When beef is lean, a thin slice of pork placed on top of roast is an excellent substitute. Put into hot oven 400 degrees for the first 10 minutes to seal juice. Lower temperature to 325 degrees and continue to cook slowly. This prevents shrinkage and helps to retain juice. Allow 20-25 minutes per pound for rare roast; 25 minutes per pound for medium and about 30 minutes per pound for a well done roast. When roast is frozen, remove from refrigerator one-half hour to cut down on roasting time. If desired, serve Yorkshire pudding.

Yorkshire Pudding: Sift 1 cup flour, and 1 tsp. salt. Mix 1 cup milk and 2 well beaten eggs; add to dry ingredients and beat until smooth. One-half hour before serving drain off surplus fat from roaster, leaving about ¼ cup in pan. Place roast to one side of pan; increase heat to 400 degrees and pour batter on other side of pan. Bake 30 minutes, or, put drippings into an 8-inch square pan, pour in batter and bake.

When cooking a large roast a favorite method is as follows: Marinate thin slices of pork in same marinade as for Brazilian Turkey. With point of sharp knife make deep slits through top and on side of roast. In these slits insert the pork slices. This tenderizes and flavors the meat. Unroll a Rolled Roast and line with these marinated pork slices; reroll and tie. Venison done in this way is delicious.

Pot Roast of Beef (with or without Vegetables)
4 to 5 lbs. beef (Chuck, Round or Rump of Beef.)

Dredge meat lightly with flour, salt and pepper. Melt about 3 tbsps. fat in skillet and sear the meat well on both sides. Add about ½ cup water and 1 or 2 bay leaves. Cover closely and simmer (do not boil) for 3 hours or longer, until meat is tender, replenishing the water when necessary. If vegetables are used, add carrots, onions, potatoes and continue cooking until vegetables are done. Thicken gravy with a little flour. If a sour-sweet gravy is preferred, add 1 tsp. sugar, 1½ tsps. lemon juice or vinegar. To vary the gravy and flavor, use tomatoes or tomato juice in place of the water.

Delicious Pickle for Beef
Make a common pickle to float a medium-sized potato. Put meat in this for 30 hours. Drain well. Make the following pickle and boil for a few minutes:

1 quart coarse salt	1 tbsp. saltpeter
1 lb. white sugar	1½ buckets water

When this pickle is cold, add meat and weight down so that it is entirely covered with the pickle. Store in a cold place.

Beef Stew
Cut stewing beef in small pieces. Brown nicely in a little hot fat, adding salt and pepper. More salt may be added later. If a dark stew is preferred, flour the meat before browning. Barely cover meat with water. Cover pot tightly and simmer slowly until meat is almost tender, adding cut up vegetables long enough before meat is tender, so that vegetables are not overdone (about 35-40 minutes). Suggested vegetables are carrots, parsnips, turnip, onions, potatoes. A little summer savory or marjoram added, when vegetables are nearly cooked, greatly improves the flavor. Stew may be thickened with a little flour, or served with dumplings.

Dumplings:

2 cups flour	2 tbsps. shortening
4 tsps. baking powder	1 cup milk
½ tsp. salt	Onion juice (optional)

Mix and sift dry ingredients. Work in shortening with pastry blender. Add milk gradually and with a knife mix to a soft dough. Drop spoonfuls of the dough on the stew mixture (liquid should not come above vegetables), allowing space for dumplings to rise. Cover pot closely and don't peek for 12-14 minutes. Lift dumplings out carefully on a platter and serve with stew.

Note: For Veal Stew, substitute veal for beef.

Braised Brisket No. 1

Braise a thick end of fresh brisket until nicely browned. Put into baking dish and season well, on both sides, with salt and pepper. Sprinkle some salt on bottom of dish. Cover brisket with a layer of sliced onions. Bake 3 or 4 hours in a slow oven 325 degrees.

Braised Brisket No. 2

3 lbs. brisket	1 carrot, chopped
Drippings for frying	1 tbsp. chopped parsley
2 tbsps. butter	½ cup diced celery
1 onion, chopped	1 cup canned tomatoes
	Salt and pepper

Cut meat in cubes and brown in hot drippings, or cook meat whole and brown as in preceding recipe. Remove meat from frying pan and put into baking dish or in skillet to complete cooking on top of stove. Rinse frying pan with ⅓ cup of water and pour this over the meat. Cover tightly and cook slowly for 2 hours. Melt the butter and brown the onion and carrot in it. Add parsley, celery and tomatoes. Heat thoroughly. Add seasonings. Pour this sauce over the meat and continue cooking for 1 hour longer.

Beefsteak and Kidney Pie

1 small beef kidney
1 lb. round steak
1 medium-sized onion,
    chopped
3 cups hot water
1 tsp. salt
¼ tsp. pepper

1 bay leaf (optional)
6 tbsps. flour
⅓ cup cold water
½ lb. mushrooms, sliced
    (optional)
Plain pastry or biscuit dough

Soak kidney in lukewarm salted water (1 tbsp. salt to 4 cups water), for 1 hour. Drain and cut off all membranes. Cut kidney and steak in 1-inch square pieces. Roll in flour and brown in a little hot butter or drippings. When meat is browned a little, add onions and stir until onions are a golden brown. Pour the hot water over the meat, onions and mushrooms, if used. Add seasoning and cook slowly until meat is tender. Thicken with flour blended with the cold water and, if necessary, add extra seasoning. Put into casserole and top with rolled out pastry or biscuit dough. Cut slits in top for steam to escape, and bake in oven 425 degrees for 35 minutes. A little diced carrot and celery may be added about one-half hour before meat is tender.

Broiled Steak

1 Porterhouse or sirloin steak
Salt and pepper

Select a steak 1½ inches thick. Heat broiler for 10 minutes with regulator set at 550 degrees. Place steak on broiler rack, about 4 inches from heat. For rare steak broil from 7 to 8 minutes, season with pepper and salt; turn and broil on other side for same length of time. Season, and place a small piece of butter on each serving. Serve at once.

Pan Broiled Steak

Heat a heavy frying pan until it is sizzling hot. Place steak in hot pan and brown well on both sides. Reduce temperature and continue cooking until meat is done, about 10 minutes for a 1½ inch steak. Pour off fat as it accumulates in pan. Season with salt and pepper. Allow ½ lb. per person.

Milanese Beef or Liver

Cut round steak, about 2 lbs., in thin slices, serving size pieces. Soak for about 2 hours in marinade solution as given in Brazilian Turkey, turning occasionally. Beat 3 or 4 eggs with ¼ tsp. salt. Dip slices of marinated meat in flour, then in the beaten eggs and lastly in fine bread crumbs. Fry in cooking oil, browning on both sides. Serve with vegetables.

Roast Pork

Select a Loin Roast of Pork, Center Cut of Fresh Ham, Shoulder Roast or Spare Ribs of Pork.

Place roast fat side up in pan. Season well with salt and pepper. Cook in oven preheated to 350 degrees, allowing 40-45 minutes to the pound. When roast is cooked remove from pan and keep in a hot place. Thicken gravy as follows:

Pour off all but about 2 tbsps. of drippings. Blend into the fat 2 tbsps. flour and stir until flour has thickened. Stir in slowly 1 cup vegetable stock or water. Season with salt, pepper or any desired seasoning. Strain gravy. Serve the roast pork dinner with applesauce or Fried Apples. A little horseradish may be added to the applesauce.

Braised Pork Chops

Heat heavy frying pan until very hot. Add about 1 tbsp. fat, or if there is fat on chops place in pan with fat side down and cook out enough fat to grease pan. Brown chops on both sides. Do not add water. Lower temperature and cook, with a cover on pan, until chops are well done, about 45 minutes.

Barbecued Spareribs

Cut spareribs in serving pieces and put into shallow baking pan. Pour over spareribs ¼ cup lemon juice and ½ cup chopped onion. Bake, uncovered, in a moderate oven 350 degrees for about 25 minutes. Make sauce as follows:

Put into saucepan and cook about 20 minutes.

2 tbsps. fat	2 tbsps. vinegar
1 cup chili sauce or	1 tbsp. Worcestershire sauce
¼ cup catsup and 1 cup tomato juice	1 tsp. dry mustard
½ cup water	1 tsp. salt
2 tbsps. brown sugar	½ tsp. paprika

Pour sauce over the spareribs, and continue baking for 1½ hours, basting frequently.

Roast Veal

Select Rolled Shoulder for a good veal roast.

Season well with salt and pepper and place in roaster, fat side up. Lay slices of salt or fresh pork or bacon over the top and roast at 325 degrees, allowing about 30 minutes per pound. Allow 10 minutes longer per pound for a rolled roast. Veal, although tender, requires longer cooking than beef. Always cook veal until well done.

Breaded Veal Cutlets

Follow recipe for Breaded Lamb Chops.
To vary, brown cutlets on both sides, cover with tomato sauce or tomato soup and cook in the same way.

Veal Casserole

Cook veal with a small amount of onion and about 2 bay leaves until meat is very tender. Remove all bones and fat and cut in small pieces for serving. Coat well with flour and brown in hot fat; drain, and place in casserole. Cover with canned mushroom soup diluted with a little of the meat stock. Sprinkle well with buttered crumbs, and brown in oven. Peas or finely diced cooked carrots added to the gravy gives additional taste and color.

Jellied Veal

Cover veal shoulder with water. Add salt, a few peppercorns and 1 bay leaf. Boil slowly until meat is tender. Strain stock and boil down until it jells. Add chopped veal, some chopped celery, green pepper, cooked peas, and if preferred, some hard boiled chopped eggs. A little seasoning sauce may be added. A little mint is quite acceptable. Pour into mould and chill until firm.

Roast Leg of Lamb

If frozen, remove leg of lamb, from refrigerator one half-hour before cooking. Without removing the fell, season with salt and pepper and rub with a cut lemon. Roast in slow oven 300 degrees, allowing about 35 minutes to the pound. Serve with thickened gravy or with unthickened gravy and mint sauce.

Variations: Cover meat with pineapple slices 1 hour before meat is done. Brush with melted butter so that pineapple browns nicely, or, baste lamb with vinegar seasoned with finely cut mint leaves.

Lamb Stew

Cut stewing lamb in about 2-inch square pieces. Roll in seasoned flour and brown in a little hot fat. Add boiling water to cover and simmer until nearly cooked, about 2 hours. Add cut up vegetables (carrots, turnip, onions and potatoes). Simmer slowly until done. Season to taste.

Fried Lamb Chops

Grease hot frying pan with a little fat. When pan is very hot, put in chops and brown quickly on both sides. Do not cover. Season on both sides with salt and pepper. Reduce heat and cook slowly until done, depending on the thickness of the chops. Keep pouring off excess fat, if any.

Breaded Lamb Chops

Dip each chop in slightly beaten egg diluted with 1 tbsp. water, then in finely rolled bread crumbs, before frying.

Curried Lamb or Chicken

Simmer the following ingredients for 10 minutes: 1 tbsp. butter, 2 tbsps. curry powder, 1 tbsp. grated onion and ¼ chopped celery. Pour boiling water over ½ cup (scant) raisins. Combine 2 cups White Sauce and 1 cup gravy. Add to this 2 cups finely cut cooked meat (lamb or chicken), 1 medium-sized finely chopped apple, ½ cup coconut, 1 small banana mashed, 2 tbsps. lemon juice, salt and pepper to taste, pinch ginger. Add raisins and curry mixture.

Roast Beef, Steak, Pot Roast or Roast Lamb is greatly improved if kept overnight in the following mixture, turning occasionally:

Equal quantities of White wine and vinegar
    (½ cup of each)
1 garlic clove, crushed
Salt and pepper to taste
1 bay leaf (for lamb use mint leaf in place of bay
    leaf).

Whole Baked Ham

Wash ham and place in roaster, fat side up. Bake in slow oven 300 degrees, allowing 25 minutes per pound for a large ham and about 30 minutes per pound for a small or half ham. When about ⅔ done, remove rind and spread with 1 tbsp. prepared mustard. Pour off fat from pan. Mix ¼ cup vinegar and 1 cup water and put into bottom of pan. Baste ham often and when almost done remove from oven and score fat in diamond shapes; stick a whole clove in each diamoned and rub surface with dry mustard and brown sugar mixed together. Bake for about 20 minutes longer or until nicely browned. Serve plain or with Raisin Sauce.

Baked Ham Slice

½ cup brown sugar   ¼ cup vinegar
1 tbsp. dry mustard   1 slice ham, about 1½ inches thick
1 tbsp. flour

Make a paste of above ingredients: add 1 cup pineapple juice or 1 cup hot water. Put slice of ham into baking dish and cover with sauce. Bake at 350 degrees for 1½ hours, basting frequently. Serve with baked or glazed potatoes. A nice variation is to cover the ham with thin slices of orange or pineapple about 10 minutes before cooking time is up, sprinkle with brown sugar, and baste with sauce until brown.

Suggested Glazes for Baked Ham:
1 cup brown sugar, juice and grated rind of orange.
1 cup brown or white sugar, ½ cup maraschino cherry juice.
1 cup brown sugar, 1 tablespoon dry mustard.

Baked Ham in Milk

1 tsp. dry mustard   1 slice ham, 2 inches thick
4 tbsps. brown sugar   Milk

Mix mustard and brown sugar together and spread over ham. Place in casserole and add enough milk to barely cover ham. Bake in oven 300 degrees for 1 hour.

Boiled Ham

Wash ham well and put into pot. Add hot water to within 1 inch of top of ham. Add ½ cup vinegar, 1 bay leaf, 2 large carrots, a little brown sugar, (1 tbsp.) a few peppercorns, and if preferred, some whole cloves. Simmer ham, allowing 30 minutes to the pound for one of medium size. Let cool in liquid as this makes it more tender and flavorful. Or, allow less time for cooking and finish baking in oven, using the brown sugar mixture as for baked ham and replacing the liquid with stock from cooking ham.

Bacon

To cook bacon place slices on wire rack or cake cooler, place rack over a shallow pan in oven 400 degrees and let crisp. This takes about 12 minutes and does not need to be turned.

To fry bacon, place in cold frying pan over low heat. Cook slowly to desired crispness, turning frequently. Pour off fat, occasionally. Drain on absorbent paper.

Bacon and Eggs

Fry bacon and when crisp remove to platter. Break the eggs, separately, into the bacon fat and cook until set.

Liver and Bacon

Fry bacon as directed. Drain on absorbent paper and keep in a hot place. Lay slices of liver (do not parboil) in hot bacon fat and season with salt and pepper. Turn occasionally and brown on both sides. Cook only until center of liver is done. Serve with or without fried onions.

Tongue

1 beef tongue	1 large carrot
1 large onion, sliced	2 stalks celery
2 tsps. salt	2 bay leaves
4 peppercorns	

Wash tongue; cover with hot water. Add seasonings and vegetables; cook about 3 hours. Cool in liquid. Remove skin and tissue. Slice and serve plain or with horseradish or any desired sauce. While cooling, the tongue may be pressed tightly into dish to mould in desired shape.

Beef or Calf's Heart

Cut the heart open and wash well with cold water. Remove arteries and veins. Drain well for 1 hour or more. Stuff the pocket with the following dressing:

2 cups fine bread crumbs	Salt and pepper to taste
1 medium-sized onion, chopped	Summer savory, marjoram or any seasoning
2 tbsps. butter	Liquid drained from the heart

Blend dry ingredients and use just enough liquid to make moist. Sew up tightly and place in roaster or baking dish. Add hot water to a depth of ½ inch, cover and bake at 325 degrees for 2 hours or longer. Thicken liquid for gravy with flour, using 1 tbsp. flour for each cupful of liquid. For a nice variation, instead of hot water, use 1 can of consomme. A little water may be added, if necessary.

Rabbit Pot Pie

Thoughts of my childhood and school days are closely associated with this pot of steaming goodness.

Wash meat well and cut in pieces. Cover with cold water and let cook for about one-half hour. Add 1 tsp. salt, some diced carrots and onions. When carrots begin to get tender add some potatoes, cut in pieces. Add a little summer savory (1 tsp.), more salt to taste and just before potatoes are done add dumplings made as follows:

Sift together 2 cups flour, 4 tsps. baking powder, ½ tsp. salt. Cut in with a knife 1 or 2 tbsps. shortening. Add 1 cup milk gradually and mix to a soft dough. Toss on floured board and roll lightly to ½-inch thickness. Cut in rounds or squares and put dumplings into pot, on top of meat and vegetables. Cover pot closely and boil for 12 minutes. Do not lift cover while dumplings are cooking. The dumplings may be seasoned by adding pepper, paprika, onion juice or parsley.

Baked Rabbit

Sprinkle serving size pieces with seasoned flour and brown on both sides in a little hot fat. Place in baking dish, cover with a thin layer of sliced onions and pour over this 1 cup sour cream. Bake, covered, in oven 350 degrees until meat is tender. Add more seasoning, if necessary.

Fried Rabbit

Wash meat and wipe dry. Cut in serving pieces. Dip pieces in seasoned flour and brown in hot fat. Lower heat and cook, tightly
covered, until meat is tender, about 1 hour or longer. If necessary,
add a little water.

Sweetbreads

Wash and cook sweetbreads. Drop in boiling water to which has
been added 1 tsp. salt and 1 tbsp. vinegar for every quart of water
used. Simmer about 25 minutes. Drain, and cover with cold water.
Drain; remove membrane. These are now ready for immediate use,
or store in refrigerator, and use in various ways.

Fried Sweetbreads: Dip cooked sweetbreads in melted butter and fry
until brown, about 12 minutes. Serve with Mushroom Sauce on
toast or with mushroom soup.

Creamed Sweetbreads: Make a Medium White Sauce. Add chopped,
cooked sweetbreads. Serve on toast or in patty shells. The addition of
sauted mushrooms, peas, or any diced leftover meat makes this a
good luncheon dish.

Broiled Sweetbreads: Parboil sweetbreads until white; chill in cold
water. Split sweetbreads. butter, season with salt and pepper, and
broil slowly until nearly done. Place in a pan with a little butter and
finish cooking in oven. In the meantime heat slices of ham in
broiler, and saute some mushrooms over a slow fire. Place ham on a
piece of toast and cover with sweetbreads and mushrooms. Top with
a sauce made of the butter used in cooking the sweetbreads and
mushrooms, blended with a little lemon juice and finely chopped
parsley.

Tripe

Tripe is the inner lining or perhaps better known as the first stom-
ach of meat animals, generally beef, and that part known as the
honeycomb is considered the choicest. According to the old folk
tripe could not be challenged for its tastiness and delicacy. Simmering in water is the first step in the preparation of tripe. It can be
bought fresh, pickled, or canned. Pickled tripe requires a shorter
period of simmering, about 2 hours. For fresh tripe, allow 4 hours
for simmering whole, or cut in strips and lessen simmering time to
2 hours.

Fried Tripe (Fresh or Pickled): Drain, dry and cut tripe in serving size pieces. Dip each piece in batter made as follows:

Sift together 1½ cups flour, 1 tsp. baking powder, ¼ tsp. salt, ¼ tsp. paprika. Beat 1 egg, add 1¼ cups milk and mix with dry ingredients, or, dip pieces in slightly beaten egg to which has been added 1 tbsp. water, roll in fine cracker crumbs and fry in deep fat heated to 390 degrees until a delicate brown. If preferred, fry in butter in a heavy frying pan, on top of stove, until nicely browned on both sides.

Stewed Tripe: Cut prepared tripe in strips. Saute in butter until lightly browned some chopped onion, finely chopped green pepper, some sliced carrot, and a small garlic clove. Add savory seasonings to give it an individual taste. Add tripe, 2 tsps. vinegar or lemon juice. Sprinkle over this 1 tbsp. flour. Pour over all ingredients 1 cup boiling water and add more salt, if necessary. Cover and simmer for about 30 minutes.

Tripe on Toast: Cut prepared tripe in small squares (1½-inch). Boil some finely chopped onion in as little water as possible, add to Medium White Sauce. Add the tripe, and a little lemon juice. Cook for 20 minutes. Serve on toast. Garnish with finely minced parsley.

Head Cheese

Remove eyes, ears, brains, snout and fat from calf's or pig's head and soak meat in cold water, for a little while, to extract the blood. (A Scottish friend told me that in her home the ears, eyes and brains were utilized in the making of this old time favorite). Wash the meat well and cover with cold water to which has been added about 1 tsp. salt. Simmer until meat begins to fall from the bones. Drain, reserving stock. Separate the meat from the bones. Cut meat in small pieces, add more salt to taste, a little pepper, and your favorite seasoning herbs. Cover well with the stock and cook for ½ hour. Pour into mould and cover with a cloth. Put weight on top. Chill, slice and serve.

Scouse (Old Time Breakfast and Luncheon Dish)

Dice salt or fresh beef in 1-inch cubes. Cover with water and cook for 1 hour. Add chopped onion, diced potatoes, salt and pepper to taste. Cook until potatoes are done, adding more water and seasoning, if necessary. Before removing from stove thicken with about 2 tbsps. flour and water enough to mix to a smooth paste.

Corned Beef and Cabbage

Select Plate Beef or Boneless Corn Brisket. Put into pot with hot water and cook until nearly tender. Add cabbage, quartered, and cook about 45 minutes or until soft. Other vegetables may be added, but added so as to allow ample time for cooking each one.

Pickled Beans Dinner

Use garden fresh beans, picked when tender and stringless. Make a brine to float an egg. Snip ends from beans, wash and put into crock. Cover with brine. Keep a weight on so that beans are completely covered. An excellent method is to put beans into a clean flour sack and immerse sack in brine. This prevents any scum from forming on beans. More beans, when suitable for picking, may be added to the brine.

Preparation: Soak beans overnight. Drain and cook as for Boiled Sauerkraut, using same cut of meat.

Note: These beans may also be cooked and used as fresh beans but more soaking may be necessary to remove salt.

Hodge-Podge

Carrots	Small new potatoes
Onion	Butter and cream
New green beans and peas	Salt and pepper

Cover carrots and onion with boiling water. Add pepper and salt, allowing 1 tbsp. salt to 1 quart of water. Add other vegetables, giving each one just time enough to cook. Watch the water and use as little as possible. When vegetables are cooked, add butter and cream or dice salt pork, fry to a golden brown, and add the cream. Pour over vegetables. Broad beans, if used, should be cooked separately and added when ready to serve.

Boiled Sauerkraut Dinner

Select Sweet Pickled Shoulder or Braising Ribs of Beef. Cook until meat begins to get tender. Scald sauerkraut by pouring boiling water over it; drain at once. Put sauerkraut into pot with meat. Add 1 tsp. sugar and continue cooking until meat is tender, about 1½ hours. Serve with fluffy mashed potatoes.

*Years ago people were not regarded as good provid-
ers unless they had in the cellar, at least a half barrel
or more of sauerkraut, turnip kraut, pickled pork
and beef, as well as salt herring and salt cod. It
sounds unbelievable, but true, nevertheless, that the
brine which forms in the sauerkraut rises and falls
with the phases of the moon. When the sauerkraut
was "cut in" apples were buried in it, and these,
when seasoned, were considered a special treat. In
the autumn when pigs were slaughtered, a consid-
erable amount of sausage and puddings was made.
The surplus sausage was either dried or pickled for
winter use, as well as to prevent spoilage.*

Sauerkraut and Bacon

2½ lbs. sauerkraut
6 or 7 slices of bacon
1 onion

Scald sauerkraut and drain immediately. Fry or broil about 4 slices of
bacon and cut in pieces. Fry onion slightly in bacon fat; add bacon
and onions to the sauerkraut. Stir all together and in the center of
pot place 2 or 3 slices of uncooked bacon. Pour over this about 1 cup
water. Cook slowly for about 2 hours, adding more water, when
necessary, to keep from scorching.

Baked Sauerkraut with Spareribs

Brown spareribs, in a little fat. Place sauerkraut, which has been
scalded and drained, in baking dish. Sprinkle with brown sugar.
Add ½ cup water and arrange spareribs on top. Cover dish and cook
in moderate over 350 degrees for about 2 hours.

Variation: Use sliced ham in place of spareribs.

Baked Sauerkraut with Salt Pork

Scald sauerkraut and drain. Place in baking dish. Add 1 tsp. sugar
and a little water, according to quantity of sauerkraut used. Place
over this thin slices of salt pork and sprinkle liberally with black
pepper. Bake, uncovered, in oven 350 degrees until pork is nicely
browned and then cover to complete baking. Stir occasionally and
add a little water to keep it from becoming too dry. The addition of
some grated raw potato makes this dish very good.

Variations: In place of salt pork use sausage or frankfurters.

Turnip Kraut

Use same cut of meat as for cooking sauerkraut. Pare turnip and cut in long narrow strips, about ¼-inch wide. When meat has cooked for ½ hour add turnip, water enough to nearly cover, 2 tbsps. sugar or more, ⅓ cup vinegar, pepper and more salt, if needed. Cook until meat and turnip are tender.

Boiled Dinner

4 lbs. cornded beef brisket	4 or 5 onions
6 or 8 carrots, quartered	1 small head cabbage
6 potatoes, quartered	Salt to taste
1 medium-sized yellow turnip, cut in pieces	

Cover meat with cold water and bring to boiling point. Lower heat and simmer gently for 3 or 4 hours. About 1 hour before meat is cooked, add vegetables and salt. Skim off any fat before adding the vegetables.

Seven Layer Dinner

1. Layer of sliced raw potatoes
2. Layer of sliced raw carrots
3. Layer of sliced raw onion
4. Layer of cooked rice (½ cup or more)
5. One can of peas, including juice
6. Layer of beef or pork sausages
7. One can of tomato soup

Cook in covered casserole for about 2 hours in 350° oven. Remove cover the last half hour of cooking. Use salt and pepper to taste.

Note: size of can of peas and tomato soup depend on quantity of vegetables used.

Poultry

There are very few creatures
Of which it can be said,
May be eaten before they are born,
And after they are dead.

Roast Turkey or Chicken

Clean bird thoroughly and wash with cold water. Dry inside and out with a cloth. Rub the inside with a little salt, if desired, a cut lemon, and fill loosely with the following dressing:

4 cups bread crumbs
1 medium-sized onion,
    chopped
½ cup melted butter
1 tsp. salt

Seasoning to taste (summer
    savory, marjoram, sage,
    thyme)
Hot water enough to make moist

Sew up incision or secure with skewers. Truss the bird so that the wings are bent behind the back and the legs are close to the body or tie these to the body to keep from becoming too dry. Grease well with butter, rub with salt and put into roaster, breast side up. Roast in oven 325 degrees until breast is nicely browned; turn breast down, cover roaster and baste frequently, with pan drippings, until tender. Allow about 25 minutes per pound for a bird under 15 pounds or 20 minutes per pound for a larger bird.

Note: The same method may be used for roasting duck or goose. When roasting goose pour off excess fat as it accumulates.

Roast Turkey, Brazilian Style

Prepare turkey for roasting, as directed. Make a mixture of ½ cup vinegar, ½ cup white wine, juice of ½ lemon, chopped onion, 1 crushed garlic clove, 1 bay leaf, pepper and salt to taste. Score turkey well with the point of a sharp knife to enable the mixture to penetrate. Put into roaster, pour the mixture over it, and let stand from 10-12 hours, basting or turning turkey several times. This tenderizes it and gives a delectable flavor. Stuff turkey with a dressing made as follows:

Boil, until tender, the giblets and heart. Cut in very small pieces, and with onions, a little garlic and salt, saute in butter. Add a few tomatoes, peeled and seeded. After these ingredients are sauted, add bread crumbs, pieces of bacon, some chopped boiled eggs and a few sliced olives. Mix well.

Fried Chicken

Cut chicken in serving pieces. Wash and dry well. Shake pieces in a paper bag containing 1 cup flour, 2 tsps. salt, ¼ tsp. pepper, ½ tsp. each celery salt and paprika. Place in a heavy skillet in ½ inch of fat (part butter and part cooking oil), turn to brown evenly. Reduce heat, cover tightly and cook slowly until tender. If necessary, add a little water. Uncover during the last 10 minutes of cooking to re-crisp, or, dip the seasoned pieces of chicken in a Fritter Batter, drop in deep fat at 360 degrees and fry until a rich golden brown. Serve immediately.

Fritter Batter: Beat 2 eggs, stir in ½ cup milk. Sift together and beat in 1 cup flour, 1 tsp. baking powder, 1 tsp. salt. Beat in 1 tsp. melted fat or salad oil.

Chicken Baked in Cream

1 chicken, cut in large pieces	1 onion, finely chopped
1 tsp. salt	1 green pepper, seeded and
⅛ tsp. pepper	chopped
1 tbsp. flour	1 cup diced uncooked carrot
¼ cup fat	1½ cups sour cream

Toss chicken pieces in seasoned flour. Sear in hot fat until crisp and golden brown; place pieces in casserole. Saute onion and chopped pepper in remaining fat left in pan; sprinkle on top of chicken. Add carrot and sour cream; cover tightly. Bake in moderate oven until tender, about 2 hours.

Variations: Fifteen minutes before chicken is removed from oven add ½ cup mushrooms, canned or fresh. This makes a most delectable gravy.

Cut up chicken and fry until nicely browned. Put into casserole with cubed uncooked carrot and pour over this 1 tin of mushroom or cream of celery soup, 1 tin of milk or chicken stock and bake at 350 degrees for 1½-2 hours.

Chicken Casserole No. 1

Put in the bottom of casserole a layer of dry onion soup mix. Over this a layer of uncooked long grain rice. Spread on top of it chicken breasts or pieces. Pour over 1 can mushroom soup, using enough milk to make it quite moist and good. Bake in moderate oven until chicken is tender. Serve with broccoli. An excellent luncheon dish.

Chicken Casserole No. 2

2 cups diced cooked chicken   ½ cup diced celery
1 tin peas drained   1 tin mushroom or cream of
2 tbsps. milk   chicken soup
                               Salt and pepper to taste

Mix all together and put into buttered casserole. Cover well with potato chips and bake in moderate oven until chips are slightly browned.

Green Shutters Chicken Pie

Cut up cooked chicken in small pieces and put into rectangular or square dish. Add chopped onion , celery, green pepper, cooked diced carrot, fresh or canned peas. Season with salt, pepper, chopped parsley, seasoning salt and curry. Add left over chicken gravy and water or vegetable stock to nearly cover. Thicken with a little flour. Put into oven and cook about 30 minutes, stirring occasionally. Cover with rolled out pastry and brush with a little milk or cream. Make several slashes in pastry for steam to escape. Brown in oven 400 degrees and serve hot. Cut in squares.

Individual Chicken Pie

Line individual pie pans with rich pastry. Place in the bottom of each pan about 1 tbsp. finely chopped celery. Add some chopped onion and diced cooked chicken or turkey. Fill to the brim with well seasoned chicken gravy. This is important, as the gravy is absorbed in the cooking. The addition of a little celery or seasoned salt improves the flavor. Cover with pastry and slash generously to allow steam to escape. Bake until nicely browned in oven 400 degrees. Serve hot with baked potato and any vegetable salad. These pies, if removed from pans when cooked, may be kept in refrigerator and reheated quite nicely.

Chicken Souffle

Melt 3 tbsps. butter; blend in 3 tbsps. flour. Add 1 cup milk gradually and cook until thick. Combine with ¼ cup grated cheese, 1 cup cooked diced chicken, 1 tsp. salt, ⅛ tsp. pepper. Beat 3 egg whites until they stand in peaks. Beat the 3 egg yolks until thick and lemon colored. To the egg yolks add the chicken mixture and carefully fold into the beaten egg whites. Turn into well buttered 8-inch casserole, sprinkle with paprika, and bake in moderate oven about 45 minutes.

Chicken Turnovers

Mince leftover chicken quite fine; add salt, pepper and desired seasoning. Mix with White Sauce. Roll out pastry to about ⅛-inch thickness and cut in rounds or squares. Place as much of the chicken mixture in the center as each one will hold. Moisten edges with milk or water and fold to shape crescents or triangles. Brush each with melted butter, milk or cream and bake about 20 minutes in oven 450 degrees. Serve hot.

Variation: Use minced meat, well seasoned, or ground ham, suitably seasoned, the same way.

Chicken Wings

Prepare sauce by combining ¼ cup soy sauce, ½ tsp. salt, ½ cup pineapple juice, 2 tbsps. sugar, ½ tsp. ground ginger, 1 tbsp. lemon juice, 6 drops Tobasco sauce, garlic salt or crushed garlic clove. Dip chicken wings in sauce and place in baking dish, basting with the remainder of the sauce while cooking. Use a moderately hot oven and cook until tender.

Chicken a la King

1 tbsp. butter or margarine
½ tsp. salt
6 tbsps. flour
1 cup sliced mushrooms
2 tbsps. chopped green pepper
½ tsp. celery salt

¾ cup milk
¾ cup light cream
1 cup chicken stock
2 cups cooked chicken, diced
1 tbsp. chopped parsley
1 tbsp. finely chopped pimiento

Melt butter, add mushrooms, green pepper, and saute for 5 minutes on low heat, stirring occasionally. Mix flour and seasonings together and add gradually to butter to make a roux, stirring constantly. Add milk, cream, and chicken stock slowly, continuing to stir until sauce thickens. Add chicken, parsley, pimiento, a pinch of cayenne pepper, adjusting seasonings to taste. Increase flour or cream to achieve desired thickness. Serve with rice.

Vegetables

Beans, carrots, corn and peas,
Beets, potatoes, take all of these
And the way that you do them,
Boil, fry or stew them;
They must be well seasoned to please.

Potatoes

Baked Potatoes: Select potatoes of uniform size. Scrub well. Grease with butter or drippings and bake in a hot oven until tender, the time depending on size and variety of potatoes. To reduce baking time, potatoes may be parboiled about 10 minutes. When potatoes are about half done, puncture with a fork to let the steam escape.

French Fried Potatoes: Wash, peel and cut potatoes in lengthwise strips, ¼-inch thick. Dry well. Fry, a small amount at a time, in deep fat 390 degrees until tender and a nice golden brown. Drain well and serve hot.

Potato Chips: Follow recipe for French Fried potatoes but cut or grate potatoes in very thin slices.

Parsleyed Potatoes: Small new potatoes are best. Peel cooked potatoes and dip, until coated, in a mixture of melted butter and minced parsley.

Glazed Potatoes: Select medium-sized potatoes. Boil and peel. Roll potatoes in slightly beaten egg yolk and bake in hot oven until golden brown.

Scalloped Potatoes No. 1: Peel potatoes; wash and cut in thin slices. Put into casserole a layer of sliced potatoes and a layer of thinly sliced onion. Season with pepper and salt, and sprinkle each layer with flour. Repeat layers and seasoning. Pour over this milk to come within a half-inch of top of potatoes. Dot liberally with butter, and bake in moderate oven for about $1\frac{1}{2}$ hours or until potatoes are tender. Potatoes may be covered for the first half hour. In place of the butter, several slices of bacon may be put on top of potatoes.

Scalloped Potatoes No. 2: Boil and slice potatoes. Make a Medium White Sauce. Add some finely minced parsley and chopped onion. Put potatoes into casserole, pour the sauce over this, and bake until thoroughly heated through.

French Fried Sweet Potatoes: Slice as for Potato Chips. Put into vinegar to preserve color. Dry well and deep fry.

Sweet Potatoes in Orange Cups: Remove the pulp from oranges; discard white membrane. Mash boiled sweet potatoes and mix with cream, salt and a little brown sugar (1 tbsp.). Add the orange pulp and fill orange cups with the mixture. Place on top of each one a marshmallow, or cover with brown sugar. Bake in moderate oven for about 20 minutes.

Kartoffelbrei (Creamed Potatoes)

Wash and slice potatoes. Cook and drain off most of the water. Add a little milk, butter, salt and a touch of nutmeg. Beat until the consistency of heavy cream. Put potato mixture into serving dish. Saute some finely chopped onion in butter, or if preferred, some chopped fried bacon, and pour over potatoes. Decorate top of dish with finely minced parsley, or saute some Zweiback crumbs in a little butter to make a good topping. This dish is internationally known as Puree.

Any left over kartoffelbrei may be made into kartoffelpuffer (potato patties) by adding an egg and a little flour. Form into patties and brown both sides in butter.

German Potato Pie

6 to 8 large potatoes
1 small onion, grated
3 eggs, well beaten

1 cup hot milk
6 tbsps. butter or margarine,
   melted
2½ tsps. salt, more if desired

Pare and grate potatoes. Combine with remaining ingredients, blending well. Put into well greased casserole, about 7 × 12 inches. Bake in moderate oven until set for 1 hour or a little longer. Serves 6.

Baked Stuffed Potatoes

Wash and scrub even sized, shapely potatoes. Parboil for 10 minutes. Bake in a moderate oven 350 degrees for 1 hour or until tender. Large potatoes require more baking time. When done remove from oven and cut a thin slice off the flat side. With a spoon carefully remove as much of the inside as you can without breaking the skin. Add to it the following:

2 tbsps. butter
1 egg, beaten slightly
2 tbsps. minced onion

Salt to taste
¼ tsp. pepper
1 tbsp. minced parsley

Blend these ingredients with a fork, fill potato shells quite full and grate a little cheese over top of each. Put the potatoes into oven or on broiler at 400 degrees to brown.

Note: The potato shells may be filled with minced leftover meat, finely chopped celery, green pepper, or, any favorite seasoning added to the potato pulp. For a vegetable filling use less potato and add peas, diced cooked carrot or celery, with seasoning to taste. The potato, mashed with butter, peas and asparagus also makes a good filling. These shells may be filled, kept in a cold place and in readiness for your luncheon party, allowing time to reheat and brown.

Stuffed Peppers

Remove tops and seeds from peppers; parboil for 5 minutes. Drain. Saute some onion in a little fat, add finely diced or ground meat and fry until light brown. Add 1 tsp. chopped parsley, 2 cups cooked rice, ½ cup tomato soup, 1 tsp. salt, ¼ tsp. pepper and ½ tsp. curry or desired seasoning. Stuff peppers and top with buttered crumbs. Stand upright in baking dish with just enough water to keep from scorching. Bake in oven 350 degrees for 15 minutes.

Note: Leftover meat or fish with the addition of chopped parsley or celery, cooked vegetables combined with cream sauce or slightly beaten egg, make excellent fillings for peppers or tomatoes.

Stuffed Tomatoes

Cut top off tomatoes and scoop out. Saute 1 tbsp. butter, ¼ tsp. salt and 1 tbsp. flour until a golden brown. Add 1 cup milk gradually, finely cut parsley, diced cooked potatoes and drained cooked peas. Cook slowly until thick and fill tomatoes. Replace tops and place tomatoes in baking dish. Cook the pulp with a little butter and flour until thick and pour pulp mixture over tomatoes. Cover with grated cheese and buttered bread crumbs. Put into oven and brown. Nice with meat loaf.

Filling No. 2: Leftover pork or veal diced or minced and combined with chopped celery, minced onion, peas, cooked rice, seasoning and meat gravy.

Filling No. 3: Remove pulp from tomatoes; sprinkle with salt and invert for about 30 minutes. Saute a little onion in butter until brown, add tomato pulp, some soft bread crumbs, pepper and salt to taste. Add slightly beaten egg and cook a minute longer. Refill tomatoes with this mixture, sprinkle with buttered crumbs and bake in oven 350 degrees for 20 minutes.

Filling No 4: Fill tomatoes with a mixture of finely diced cold cooked parsnip and apple mixed with mayonnaise. Put top back on tomato, and serve beside any salad.

Fried Tomatoes

Cut ripe or green tomatoes in thick slices. Dip each slice in slightly beaten egg and then in dry bread crumbs, finely ground. Fry on both sides, in butter.

Baked Tomatoes

Cut tomatoes crosswise in thick slices. Place in a greased baking dish, cover with chopped onion and small green onions, parsley and salt. Sprinkle lightly with brown sugar, dot with butter and bake in moderate oven for 30 minutes.

Frozen Tomatoes

Wash tomatoes and remove any bad spots. Put into pot and stand on back of stove. Do not add any water. Let come to squashy state gradually. Put into containers, allowing 1 inch for expansion. Freeze.

Tasty Spiced Harvard Beets

1 tbsp. cornstarch	⅓ cup vinegar
2 tbsps. sugar	⅔ cup water
½ tsp. salt	4 cups cooked diced beets
¼ tsp. ground cloves	1 tbsp. butter

Mix cornstarch, sugar, salt and spice. Add vinegar and water. Cook, stirring constantly, until thickened. Add beets and simmer gently for 10 minutes. Add butter and serve hot as a vegetable.

Beets in Orange Sauce

3 cups diced cooked beets	1 tbsp. melted butter
1 small onion, finely chopped	Juice and rind of 1 orange
3 tbsps. sugar	Salt to taste
1 tbsp. vinegar	

Mix all ingredients and place in saucepan. Cover tightly and simmer for 15 minutes. Serve with roast pork, baked ham or fried chicken.

Beets in Lemon Sauce

3 cups diced uncooked beets	3 tsps. butter
1 small onion, finely chopped	Juice of ½ lemon

Saute onion in butter. Put all ingredients into tightly covered saucepan. Add salt to taste. Cook for 40 minutes or until beets are tender.

Beets and Onions

Peel uncooked beets and cut very fine. Cut onions in small pieces and saute in about 3 tsps. butter. Add beets (about 3 cups), juice of ½ lemon, and salt to taste. Cook, tightly covered, until beets are tender.

Candied Squash

Wash and dry required number of acorn or pepper squash. Cut in halves lengthwise, scoop out seeds and loosen fibres with a spoon. Put a small piece of butter in each half and sprinkle with salt, pepper, a little brown sugar and a touch of grated nutmeg. Cover the top of each squash half with a piece of foil, press foil close to sides and bake in a hot oven 400 degrees until squash is almost tender. Remove foil, baste squash halves with juice, sprinkle cut edges with more brown sugar. Return to oven and bake, uncovered, 15 minutes longer.

Candied Sweet Potatoes or Parsnips

6 medium-sized sweet potatoes   4 tbsps. butter
½ cup brown sugar   ½ tsp. salt
1 cup boiling water   2 tsps. chopped peanuts

Pare and slice potatoes or parsnips. Make a syrup of the sugar, water, butter and salt. Put potatoes into baking dish; pour syrup over potatoes. Bake in slow oven 325 degrees for 1 hour or until candied. When nearly done sprinkle with the chopped nuts and brown lightly. Orange slices and a little orange juice make a nice variation. Potatoes and parsnips may be parboiled to save time.

Fried Apples

1 apple   ½ tsp. sugar
1 egg, beaten   1½ tbsps. fat
¼ tsp. cinnamon

Core apples and cut in ¼-inch slices. Dip in egg, sprinkle with cinnamon and sugar mixture. Fry slowly in fat until tender and brown.

Fried Cucumber

Cut new cucumbers, unpared, in round slices. Dip slices in slightly beaten egg, then in flour and salt. Saute in hot fat.

Cole Slaw

Cube and fry out ½ lb. salt fat pork. Cut up 1 medium-sized head of cabbage in small pieces and add to pork fat (scraps may be used or discarded). Add about ¾ cup brown sugar, ½ cup or more vinegar, pepper to taste and more salt, if needed. Cook slowly for about 2 hours, stirring occasionally.

Cabbage with Butter

Wash 1 medium-sized new cabbage very well, leaf by leaf, keeping cabbage whole. Put into boiling salted water and cook until tender. When cooked, place in baking dish and pour over it melted butter, being careful that butter goes between each leaf. Cover with grated cheese and bread crumbs. Over this put a few spoonfuls of melted butter. Put into oven to brown. Serve whole from table. Cut in wedges, and serve with roast beef or a steak dinner.

Brussel Sprouts

Soak sprouts for 10 minutes in salted water. Drop in rapidly boiling salted water, lower heat and cook, uncovered, until tender. Drain and pour melted butter over sprouts.

Broccoli

Soak in salted water for about 10 minutes. Cook in a little water until tender, about 12 minutes. Drain, sprinkle with salt and melted butter.

Creamed Broccoli

Prepare and cook as in preceding recipe. Drain and chop quite fine. Saute a little finely chopped onion in 2 tbsps. butter. Blend in 2 tbsps. flour, and slowly stir in 1 cup milk. Add ¼ tsp. salt and a little paprika. Add broccoli and stir until mixture is well blended. Place in baking dish, sprinkle with buttered bread crumbs and some grated cheese. Bake in a hot oven 400 degrees until mixture is heated and cheese melted.

Corn on the Cob

Remove husks and silk from ears of corn. Drop in boiling water to which has been added 1 tbsp. sugar and a little salt. Boil from 6 to 10 minutes, depending on maturity of the corn. Drain, and serve with butter.

Risoto (Used as Vegetable instead of Potato)

1 cup uncooked rice, 3 cups vegetable stock or water, 5 tbsps. grated cheese, butter and finely chopped onion. Saute rice in about 2 tbsps. butter; add the stock or water and salt. Cook in tightly covered pan, without disturbing, for 30 minutes or until dry. Saute onions in 1 tbsp. butter; add onions and the cheese to rice. Mix well, but lightly, to keep rice fluffy.

Cauliflower

Break cauliflower in small flowerets and boil in enough salted water to completely cover. Drain thoroughly. Put cauliflower on a heated plate, and sprinkle with grated cheese and parsley. Cover with melted butter and toasted bread crumbs. Place in oven until cheese is melted.

Braised Red Cabbage

1 medium sized head of cabbage, finely sliced	1 bay leaf
	Salt and pepper to taste
1 medium sized onion, finely minced	2 tbsps. cider vinegar
	3 tbsps. brown sugar or red currant jelly
2 small apples, unpeeled and chopped	
4 whole cloves	

Put all ingredients in pot, bring to a boil and then continue cooking on very low heat, simmering for a couple hours. Do not add any water. Add more vinegar or sugar to taste, if desired. Add 1 cup of sweet Vermouth near end of cooking time. Excellent!

Green Bean Casserole

2 pkgs. frozen green beans	onion rings
1 can mushroom soup	cheese slices

Put beans into buttered casserole. Top with onion rings. Pour over the mushroom soup and place cheese slices on top. Cover with buttered bread crumbs and bake in moderate oven until cheese is melted and crumbs lightly browned.

String Beans with Cheese

Cook beans in salted water and drain. Saute some chopped onion in butter, add beans and before serving sprinkle with grated cheese.

Baked Filled Acorn Squash

Cook spinach and drain well. Chop quite fine and add some finely chopped onion and a dash of nutmeg. Mix with some Medium White Sauce. Prepare and bake squash halves, and while hot, fill with the creamed spinach. Garnish with narrow strips of pimiento.

Vegetable Casserole

1 cup cooked or canned peas, drained

1 cup cooked or canned green beans, drained

1 cup cooked sliced carrots

1 cup cooked diced celery

3 or 4 tbsps. grated or finely chopped onion

2 cups medium white sauce, paprika

¾ cup buttered bread or cracker crumbs

Reserve liquid from peas and use it for making sauce. Put vegetables in layers in greased casserole. Sprinkle each layer with the chopped onion. Pour sauce over vegetables. Top with buttered crumbs and a dash of paprika. Grated cheese may be used instead of the bread crumbs. Bake in 375° oven for 25 mins. Serves 6 or 8.

2. The Added Touch

Soups and Chowders

Now come little clams and listen to me,
Dig deep your homes in the sand of the sea.
If you do not, it really is true,
You may find yourself in a wonderful stew.

Green Shutters Broth

Select a good soup bone, preferably sirloin. Wash, put into pot and almost cover with boiling water; boil for about 5 minutes. Drain off. (This kills bacteria and prevents sourness). Almost cover bone with cold water and simmer gently for several hours, adding shredded or finely chopped carrots, turnip, onions, celery, barley or rice. The pods of a few new green peas washed and added give it a distinctive flavor. Any suitable vegetable oddments may be added to the soup pot. Add extra water or vegetable stock, and salt to taste. (Any water in which meat or vegetables have been cooked is "stock"). Seasoning salt, parsley and green onion tops or extra onions may be added to compliment the flavor. Serve with Croutons or Bread Sticks.

Chicken Noodle Soup

1 4-pound fowl	3 quarts water
1 large onion, chopped	3 or 4 peppercorns
4 carrots, diced	Salt and pepper to taste
2 or 3 stalks celery	

Cook fowl in the water until nearly done; add diced vegetables, seasoning, and cook until fowl is tender and vegetables cooked. Remove fowl and add noodles which have been made and left to dry for several hours. After adding noodles, boil for about 10 minutes.

Noodles: 1 egg, 1 tbsp. milk, ¼ tsp. salt, enough flour to make dough stiff enough to roll out. Roll dough in a thin rectangle and allow to dry. Roll up like jelly roll. Cut in thin shreds and separate before adding to soup.

Cream Soup Supreme

| 1 can cream of mushroom soup | 2 cans rich milk |
| 1 can aspargus tips, finely minced | |

Mix together well, using liquid from can of asparagus. Serve piping hot. A favorite.

Split Pea Soup

2 cups split peas
6 cups water
3 cups well seasoned stock

Boil peas in water for 30 minutes. Simmer until tender, about 1½ hours.

Add the stock made from a ham bone or turkey carcass. When ready to serve, add a little cream and chopped parsley.

Sauerkraut Soup

Pour boiling water over sauerkraut and cook for about 10 minutes. Drain off water. Cover with water, add diced fresh or salt meat and cook for 1 hour. Add thinly sliced potatoes, salt and pepper to taste. Brown some flour in oven, until golden in color. Stir this into some hot water, and add to soup. Cook about 5 minutes longer.

Spiced Tomato Soup

7 cups canned tomatoes	2 bay leaves
4 cups water	4 tbsps. butter
2 tbsps. sugar	⅔ cup chopped onions
4 tsps. salt	2 tbsps. chopped parsley
8 cloves	2 tbsps. flour
8 peppercorns	½ tsp. soda

Heat tomatoes, water, sugar and salt in saucepan. The cloves, peppercorns and bay leaves in a small square of cheese cloth and add to soup. Bring to a boil. Melt butter in a small saucepan, add onion and parsley and saute for about 10 minutes. Stir in flour mixture. Add soda and simmer for 30 min. Makes 8 to 12 servings.

Cabbage Soup

1 lb. hamburger
2 tbsps. cooking oil
2 large onions, chopped
1 cup chopped celery
½ green pepper, chopped
2 tbsps. sugar
1 28-oz. tin tomatoes
2 5½-oz. tins tomato paste
3 tbsps. chopped parsley

1 cup diced carrots
2 cups diced potatoes
6 cups chopped cabbage
2 small hot red peppers
2 beef bouillon cubes
2 tsps. salt, dash of pepper
4 or more cups water

Saute beef, onion, celery and pepper in heated oil until red has disappeared from meat. Combine remaining ingredients, except cabbage, and cook slowly for 1 hour, stirring frequently. Add cabbage and cook for another hour. Add water, 1 cup at a time, during cooking. This makes a substantial meal and freezes well.

Russian Borsch

4 pints stock
3-4 lbs. beetroot
½ lb. fresh cabbage
2 carrots
1 parsnip
2 stalks celery
1 large onion
½ tsp. pepper

3 tbsps. tomato puree or (¼ lb. fresh tomatoes)
2 tbsps. vinegar
1 tbsp. sugar
1-2 bay leaves
1 sprig dill or parsley
1½ tsp. salt
¼ pint sour cream

Prepare stock. Clean and shred beetroot, carrots, parsley, celery and onion. Put into saucepan, add tomatoes, sugar and enough stock with a little fat (if stock has no fat add 1-2 tbsps. butter) to cover vegetables. Simmer for 15-20 minutes, stirring from time to time, adding stock and water to prevent sticking. Add shredded cabbage, mix well and simmer another 15-20 minutes. Pour in all stock, add salt and pepper, bay leaf, 1 tbsp. vinegar and simmer until vegetables are done. To give color, keep one beetroot for last minute use and run through fine grater; combine with cupful of stock and bring to boil, simmer for 2-3 minutes with 1 tbsp. vinegar, and strain the liquid into the Borsch. Sprinkle with finely chopped parsley, dill, and sour cream.

Note: Bacon, ham and frankfurter sausages may be added, also mushrooms and slight flavoring of garlic.

Dry Bean Soup (Bohnensuppe)

1 2-lb. beef bone or 1 ham
    bone
1½ cups diced turnip
1 large onion, chopped fine
1 medium-sized carrot, diced

1½ cups dried beans (home raised
    beans, preferred)
Salt and pepper to taste

Soak beans for several hours. Cook meat or ham bone and beans slowly for two hours with enough water to cover bone. Add vegetables and cook until soft. If preferred, add 1 stalk of diced celery and cook for about 15 minutes longer. Add **ribbele** made as follows:

Add cold water, a few drops at a time, to about ¾ cup flour, stirring constantly with a spoon until mixture can be cut (using knife and fork) into shreds. Cook soup a little longer.

Potato Soup

Pare and dice about 3 large potatoes. Add 1 small chopped onion, ½ tsp. salt and cover with boiling water. Cook until potatoes are done. Put 1 qt. milk, 1 tiny bay leaf, 1 or 2 stalks celery into another saucepan and bring slowly to the scalding point. Strain this into the cooked potato and onion. If celery is omitted, season soup with celery salt.

Fish Chowder

2½ pounds fish (halibut or
    any white fish)
2 ounces salt fat pork
1 large onion
2 medium-sized potatoes

1 quart milk or cream
6 crackers
Salt and pepper

Dice pork, onion and potatoes. Boil fish in small amount of water until nearly separated from the bones. Remove skin and bones; break up any large pieces of fish. Reserve water. Fry pork in soup pot until cubes are a delicate brown. Add onion, potatoes, and fish water. When potatoes are soft, add fish, milk and cream. Heat, but do not boil. Roll crackers and add to chowder. Season to taste, and serve.

Mushaboom Chowder

2 cups milk	1 small can Sockeye Salmon
1 can mushroom soup	1 small can lobster
1¼ cup rich milk or cream	Salt and pepper to taste
1 onion, chopped	

In saucepan cook onion lightly in butter. Add other ingredients, removing skin and bones from salmon and breaking up fish in small pieces. Using liquid from fish, bring to scalding point. Serves 6 generously.

Quick Fish Chowder

Pare and cube enough potatoes to make about 2 cupfuls. Put into pot with enough water to cook, barely covered. On top of potatoes put 1 tsp. salt, 1 medium-sized chopped onion, and 2 medium-sized slices of fresh halibut or haddock fillet, washed and drained. The fish and onion will cook as quickly as the potatoes. When potatoes are soft put pot where it keeps hot but does not boil. Remove from fish, skin and bones, if any. Add a good size piece of butter, some cream and enough milk to make to desired consistency. Add more salt and pepper to taste. A few rolled cracker crumbs may be added to make a thicker chowder.

Note: Fish may be cooked in advance, and kept in refrigerator until needed. Cook fish in small amount of water; remove skin and bones. Keep fish in covered container.

Clam Chowder

1 pint clams	1 tbsp. salt
4 cups potatoes, cubed	⅛ tsp. pepper
2-inch cube salt pork	4 tbsps. butter
1 chopped onion	4 cups scalded milk
½ cup cream	6 crackers

Reserve liquor if you steam clams, using the least water possible for steaming. Saute pork in pot until a delicate brown; remove scraps. Add about 2 cups water, potatoes, onions, salt, and cook until potatoes are tender. Add clams, some of the reserved liquor, butter, milk and cream. Let stand to simmer on back of stove until ready to serve. Season with pepper and more salt, if necessary. Cracker crumbs may be added.

Corn Chowder

1 can cream-style corn
3 cups potatoes, cubed
1½-inch cube salt pork
1 chopped onion

3 cups scalded milk
2 tbsps. butter
¼ cup cream
6 crackers, rolled fine
Salt and pepper

Dice pork fine and fry to a delicate brown; remove scraps. Add about 1 cup water, potatoes and onion. Cook until potatoes are tender. Add corn, milk, butter, cream and seasonings. Let simmer on back of stove until ready to serve. Add cracker crumbs for a thicker chowder.

Salads and
Salad Dressings

The results are most impressing,
When we help with our salad dressing.

Tossed Salad

Take any quantity of lettuce or fresh crisp greens that have been thoroughly washed and dried; tear or cut in pieces and put into wooden bowl. Add grated carrot, finely shredded cabbage, some chopped celery and green pepper, onion rings or finely chopped onion. Chopped chives and parsley give added color and flavor. Chill all vegetables, except onion, until ready to serve. Using salad oil, depending on quantity of salad, use just enough to lightly coat every piece (about 1 tbsp.). This greatly improves the flavor of the salad. Then add a sprinkle of salt, garlic powder, Salad Surprise, Accent or any favorite seasoning and just enough oil dressing to mix. Do not combine salad ingredients and dressing until immediately before serving. With a fork and spoon toss lightly, but well, to distribute the flavor. If preferred, the bowl may be rubbed with a garlic clove and the garlic powder omitted. Garnish with hard boiled eggs, radishes, tomatoes, cucumber or pepper rings. For added attractiveness, dust with paprika.

Spinach Salad

1 cup mayonnaise	dash of pepper
½ cup sugar	sliced hard boiled egg
½ cup milk	fried crisp bacon, broken in bits
4 tbsps. cider vinegar	sliced onion rings
½ tsp. salt	spinach

Make dressing by combining well first six ingredients. Keeps well in tightly covered jar in refrigerator.

Crisp and shred as much spinach as required and use dressing according to quantity needed. Combine spinach with sliced onion rings, sliced cold egg and lastly the bacon.

I use part spinach, crisp dark leaf lettuce, scallions, sliced radish, parsley, for a truly delicious salad.

Frozen Summer Salad

⅔ cup sliced strawberries	2 tsps. lemon juice
1 cup diced drained canned pineapple	1 tsp. gelatin
	1 tbsp. each cold and hot water
½ cup orange sections	1 tbsp. liquid honey
½ cup seedless grapes, halved	1 cup whipping cream

Mix fruits with lemon juice and chill. Soften gelatin in cold water and dissolve in hot water. Add honey to gelatin, stir and pour over fruit. Whip cream until stiff and fold in the fruit mixture. Spoon into freezing tray and freeze until firm. Cut in squares and serve on lettuce or your favorite greens. Decorate with cherries and melon balls.

Frozen Winter Salad

Crush ⅓ cup Roquefort cheese; put through sieve and then blend with ⅓ cup cream cheese. Add 1 cup shredded cabbage, 2 tsps. lemon juice and 3 tbsps. finely chopped celery. Fold in 1 cup whipped cream and put into tray to freeze. Cut in squares and serve on lettuce. Top with salad dressing.

Ginger Ale Salad

1 tbsp. gelatin	¼ cup chopped celery
2 tbsps. cold water	½ cup seedless grapes
¼ cup ginger ale, heated	½ cup crushed pineapple
¼ cup lemon juice	½ cup chopped preserved ginger
1½ cups cold ginger ale	Cream mayonnaise

Soak gelatin in cold water; add heated ginger ale and dissolve. Stir in lemon juice and cold ginger ale. Place mixture in refrigerator to set. When it begins to stiffen, add celery and fruit. Return to refrigerator to set. Serve on lettuce beds and garnish with cream mayonnaise (1 cup whipped cream and 1 cup mayonnaise).

Cranberry and Orange Salad No.1

1 cup cranberries	2 tsps. grated orange rind
1 cup sugar	¾ cup chopped celery
1 pkg. lemon gelatin	1 can crushed pineapple
½ cup boiling water	½ cup pecan meats
1 cup orange juice	

Put cranberries through food chopper; mix with sugar and let stand for several hours, stirring to dissolve sugar. Add gelatin to boiling water and stir until dissolved. Stir in orange juice and other ingredients. Pour into mould or an 8 × 8 inch square pan. Place in refrigerator to set and serve on crisp lettuce. Garnish with a dash of mayonnaise and tiny sprig of parsley.

Cranberry and Orange Salad No. 2

Add a small quantity of finely ground raw carrots, orange pulp and a little of the grated rind (1 orange) to a can of cranberry sauce, whole berry type. Make a plain gelatin and add this to mixture. Chill until firm. Mould, as directed for preceding, recipe, or fill custard cups, and serve with mayonnaise.

Party Salad

1 pkg. lime jello
1 cup hot pineapple juice
12 or 14 large marshmallows, cut

⅔ cup apples, chopped
⅔ cup pineapple, diced
1 cup celery, finely chopped

Put jello in bowl and add the hot pineapple juice. Add marshmallows to mixture. Cool slightly and put in refrigerator. When partly chilled add apples (leaving red peel on if desired), pineapple and celery. When mixture begins to set fold in ½ cup salad dressing and ½ cup whipped cream. Place in individual moulds and chill.

Unmould on crisp lettuce and garnish with the following fruit salad dressing:

2 eggs beaten
½ cup sugar

¼ cup lemon juice
¼ cup pineapple juice

Cook in double boiler until thickened, stirring constantly. Keep in refrigerator and just before serving add ¾ cup whipped cream.

Delicious Cherry Mold

½ cup currant or cranberry jelly
2 cups water
1 6-oz. pkg. raspberry jello

½ cup sherry wine
¼ cup lemon juice
dash of salt
2 cans pitted dark sweet cherries

Combine jelly and 1 cup of the water in a saucepan and bring to a boil. Then add raspberry jello, stirring to dissolve. Remove from heat and add the other cup of water, wine, lemon juice and salt. Then add well drained cherries after jello has just started to set. Set mould in refrigerator.

Cottage Cheese Mold

1 pkg. lemon jello
1 pkg. lime jello
1⅞ cups boiling water
¾ cup milk

1 2 oz. tin crushed pineapple
1 24 oz. tub cottage cheese
1 cup Miracle Whip mayonnaise

Dissolve jello in boiling water. Add pineapple and cool. Mix together cheese, milk and Miracle Whip. Add the pineapple and jello mixture. Pour into oiled mold and chill. Turn mold out on a chilled dish and garnish.

Mushroom Mold

5 cups beef consomme   2 cups mushrooms, drained
3 pkgs. unflavored gelatin   ½ cup sherry

Dissolve gelatin in consomme and heat. Remove from stove and add mushrooms and sherry. Pour into oiled mold and chill for several hours or until firm. Unmold and garnish with endive or favorite greens and lemon twists.

Cardinal Salad Mold

1 package lemon jello   ½ tsp. salt
1 cup boiling water   ¾ cup diced celery
¾ cup beet juice   1 cup cooked diced beets
3 tbsps. vinegar   2 tsps. onion juice or grated
1 tbsp. horseradish   onion

Dissolve gelatin in boiling water. Add beet juice, vinegar, salt, onion or onion juice and horseradish. Chill until partially set. Fold in celery and beets. Pour into oiled mold. Chill until firm.

Bacon and Egg Mousse

Cut ¼ lb. side bacon in small pieces and fry until crisp. Drain on absorbent paper. Cool.

Combine in a heat proof bowl 2 tbsps. gelatin and ½ cup water; let stand for 5 minutes. Place in a pan of hot water and heat until gelatin is dissolved. Keep hot until needed.

Measure into large bowl 1 cup mayonnaise; gradually stir in 1 cup undiluted evaporated milk or light cream, ¼ cup strained lemon juice. Quickly stir in hot dissolved gelatin; stir in the cooked bacon, ½ tsp. salt, ⅛ tsp. pepper, ¼ tsp. Accent, 4 coarsely chopped hard cooked eggs, ¾ cup finely chopped celery, ¼ cup finely chopped green pepper, ½ cup cooked or canned green peas.

Chill the mixture, folding occasionally, until solids stay distributed throughout the mixture. Turn into a mold that has been brushed lightly with salad oil and rinsed with cold water. Chill until set. Garnish with pimiento. Serves 8.

Tomato Mousse

Soak 2 tbsps. plain gelatin in ½ cup cold water. Heat one 10 oz. can of cream of tomato soup and beat in one 6 oz. package of white cream cheese. Add dissolved gelatin and beat well. When thoroughly blended and cool, add ¾ cup finely minced celery, ¾ cup finely minced green pepper, ½ cup finely minced green onion and 1 cup mayonnaise. Pour into individual oiled molds; chill and unmold on crisp crinkly lettuce beds. It's delicious!

Frosted Luncheon Fruit Mold

2 3-oz. pkgs. lime flavored
  gelatin
2 cups boiling water
2 7-oz. bottles (2 cups) lemon-
  lime carbonated beverage
2 cups crushed pineapple
2 bananas, sliced

½ cup sugar
2 tbsp. all-purpose flour
2 eggs, slightly beaten
1 cup whipping cream
½ cup shredded sharp cheese
4 tbsps. grated Parmesan cheese

Dissolve gelatin in boiling water; cool. Add carbonated beverage. Chill until partially set. Drain pineapple, reserving syrup. Fold drained pineapple and banana into gelatin mixture. Turn into 8 × 8 × 2 inch baking pan. Chill until firm. Combine sugar and flour in saucepan. Stir in reserved pineapple syrup and the egg. Cook and stir over low heat until thickened. Chill. Whip cream and fold into egg mixture. Spread over gelatin. Sprinkle with grated and shredded cheese. To serve, cut into squares and serve on crisp lettuce. Makes 16 servings, Superb!

Pineapple Mint Salad

1 pkg. lime jello
1 cup hot water
½ cup canned pineapple juice

½ cup cold water
¼ tsp. mint flavoring
1 cup canned pineapple

Dissolve jello in hot water. Add the pineapple juice, cold water and mint flavoring. Chill until slightly thickened. Then fold in the pineapple which has been drained and diced. Pour mixture into mold or individual molds and chill until firm. Serve on lettuce beds. A suitable salad to serve with lamb.

Tuna or Salmon Salad

1 8-oz. can tuna or salmon
½ cup diced celery
¼ cup chopped sweet green
    pepper
1 tsp. diced pimiento
1 doz. cut up ripe olives
    (optional)

1 tsp. chopped parsley
¼ tsp. salt
⅛ tsp. pepper
1 tsp. lemon juice
¼ cup mayonnaise

Drain and flake the tuna and add all other ingredients. Combine lightly with fork. Serve on beds of crisp lettuce.

Note: Fresh tuna or salmon is preferred, if available. This salad is very nice if served on pineapple slices and sprinkled with a few shredded toasted almonds.

Lobster Salad

2 cups lobster meat
2 cups finely chopped celery
2 tbsps. chopped stuff olives
    (optional)

Juice of 1 lemon
1 head lettuce

Sprinkle lemon juice over lobster meat; add celery and olives. Mix together lightly with fork and add just enough mayonnaise to moisten. Pack salad in individual moulds and chill. Make "cups" of two crisp lettuce leaves. Place chilled mould in lettuce cups and decorate with cucumber slices and paprika.

Hot Lobster Salad

3 cups lobster, cut up
1 medium-sized onion
1 tsp. dry mustard
2 tbsps. vinegar

1 tbsp. flour
½ cup sweet cream
1 small tsp. sugar
Salt and pepper to taste

Saute onion in a little butter. Mix flour and mustard with vinegar. Add cream and sugar and pour over lobster meat. Let simmer to thicken. Serve in pastry shells.

Hot Crab Meat Salad

Make a Medium White Sauce. Mix 1 cup flaked crab meat, 2 cups diced celery, ¼ cup minced green pepper, 2 chopped hard boiled eggs and 1 tsp. salt. Add this mixture to sauce and stir well. Pour into buttered baking dish, sprinkle with buttered bread crumbs, and bake in oven 350 degrees for about 40 minutes. Serve hot in pastry shells, or in Toasted Bread Baskets.

Cucumber Salad

Peel and slice about 6 medium-sized cucumbers. Put into dish and sprinkle each layer with a little salt. Press with a heavy weight for 2 hours or longer. Drain well. Cut up some onion quite fine and add to cucumbers. Mix with the following dressing: 1 cup sour cream (slightly whipped), ½ cup (more or less) sugar, ⅓ cup vinegar, little pepper.

Note: These proportions are approximate, sugar and vinegar are added to taste.

Lettuce and Sour Cream Salad

This salad is better made with leaf lettuce. Wash lettuce in several waters. 'Ring' out and 'tear' in pieces. Mix with a dressing made of 1 cup sour cream, ½ cup sugar, ⅓ cup vinegar and ⅛ tsp. salt. If cream is thin, chill and whip it. This makes a fluffier and tastier salad.

Sauerkraut Salad

1 large tin sauerkraut, drained
¾ cup sugar
1 small red pepper, chopped
1 small green pepper, chopped

1 onion, minced
¾ cup cider vinegar
¾ cup salad oil

Mix all together. This salad keeps well in refrigerator. Celery or caraway seeds may be added, according to taste.

Marinated Tomatoes

2 or 3 large ripe tomatoes, sliced
1 cup Italian salad dressing
½ tsp. salt

½ tsp. dry mustard
¼ cup thinly sliced green onion
¼ cup minced fresh parsley

Wilted Lettuce Salad

Garden lettuce (leaf)
2 or 3 strips bacon
1 or more sweet onions

1 tbsp. sugar
¼ cup vinegar
Salt to taste

Separate lettuce leaves. Wash and drain well. Cook bacon until crisp; cut in pieces. Add sugar and vinegar to bacon and drippings; and heat well. Add lettuce leaves and thinly sliced onions; stir well. Top with chopped hard cooked egg. Serve immediately.

Chicken or Turkey Salad

3 cups cooked diced chicken or
    turkey
1 cup diced celery
⅛ tsp. Lowry's seasoned salt

Salt and pepper to taste
Cream mayonnaise
Crisp lettuce

Mix with heavy mayonnaise (mayonnaise and whipped cream) to desired consistency. Serve on crisp lettuce beds or in lettuce cups.

Pretzel Salad

1 cup crushed Pretzel sticks
⅓ cup butter
1 cup sugar

Melt butter, mix with sugar, pretzels, and bake 12 minutes at 350°. (9 × 13 inch pan preferred).

Combine 1 8-oz. pkg. cream cheese, ½ cup pulverized sugar, and 1 large tub Cool Whip. Spread on cooled pretzel crust.

Prepare 1 pkg. strawberry jello with 1 cup boiling water. When cool add 1 pkg. frozen strawberries, 1 can crushed pineapple, well drained. Spread on cream cheese layer. Keep in refrigerator, covered.

Tomato Aspic

1 large tin tomato juice
4 stalks celery
2 tsps. fresh lemon juice

1 large chopped onion
½ tsp. salt

Combine above ingredients in saucepan; bring to a boil and let simmer for about 20 minutes. Strain and pour over 3 pkgs. lemon jello. Stir until dissolved; pour into moulds or large pan 11 × 7. When set, cut in squares. Serve with a dash of mayonnaise and a tiny sprig of parsley on top.

Vegetable Aspic

Soften 2 tbsps. unflavored gelatin in ½ cup cold water, for 5 minutes. Dilute contents of 1 tin cream of tomato soup with 1 tin water; heat to boiling point and add to gelatin. Cool until slightly thickened. Blend a 3-oz. pkg. softened cream cheese with ½ cup cooked salad dressing. Stir in ¼ cup chopped green pepper, ½ cup chopped celery, ¼ cup sliced stuffed olives. Add this to gelatin and pour into mould or dish. Chill. Garnish with cold boiled egg and parsley.

Salad Accompaniments: Croutons, bread sticks, cheese balls, melon balls, celery curls, radish roses, sliced cucumbers, orange slices, stuffed prunes.

Roll cream cheese balls in chopped burnt almonds for fruit salads. Place one in the hollow of a pear or peach half.

Remove pit from plum or prune. Fill with cream cheese and place on top of pineapple slice. Serve on crisp lettuce leaves and with Fruit Salad Dressing.

Mock Mushrooms: Cut small-sized tomatoes in two. Scoop out so as to make "hats". Pour over hats a little French dressing and let stand about 30 minutes. Cook eggs hard, remove shells, and cut end off to make eggs stand. On top of each egg put a tomato hat, and with pastry decorator put mayonnaise on each egg to form a shadow. Place a "mushroom" in center of any salad or use to decorate a platter of meat.

French Dressing

4 tbsps. sugar	1 cup salad oil
4 tbsps. tomato ketchup	Juice of ½ lemon
3 tbsps. vinegar	1 onion, grated
1 tbsp. Worcestershire sauce	Pinch of mace
1 tsp. salt	½ tsp. celery seed

Put all ingredients into a jar with a screw top. This dressing will keep indefinitely in refrigerator. Shake well before using it.

Russian Dressing

½ cup Miracle Whip	1 tbsp. green pepper, cut fine
¼ cup Chili sauce	Some chopped pimiento
1 tbsp. celery, cut fine	Salt and pepper to taste

Combine ingredients. Keep in refrigerator until ready to serve.

Lem's Favorite Salad Dressing

⅔ cup sugar
3 heaping tbsps. flour
2 tsps. dry mustard
1 tsp. salt

1 cup vinegar
⅛ lb. butter
4 large eggs

Sift together the first four ingredients. Heat vinegar and butter in double boiler. Beat the eggs until thick and lemon colored; gradually add the sifted dry ingredients and then the heated vinegar and butter. Return to double boiler and cook until thick, stirring constantly. Put into airtight sealers. This keeps indefinitely in refrigerator. Dilute with mik or whipped cream.

Hilda's Salad Dressing

1 cup Mazola oil
2 cups vinegar
2 cups granulated sugar

½ cup tomato ketchup
¼ cup prepared mustard

⅛ tsp. each of celery salt, paprika, monosodium glutamate (garlic, if preferred), or any desired flavoring. Blend well and keep in airtight bottle in refrigerator. Keeps indefinitely. This is my popular dressing for tossed salad.

Quick Salad Dressing

1 can condensed milk
    (sweetened)
2 eggs
½ tsp. salt

½ tsp. dry mustard
Beat with egg beater and add
    ¾ cup vinegar.

Fruit Salad Dressing

1 cup pineapple juice
1 cup orange juice
½ cup lemon juice
1 cup sugar

3 egg yolks
1 heaping tbsp. cornstarch
1 tsp. butter

Mix juices with sugar in top of double boiler. When hot add to yolks slightly beaten and blended with cornstarch. Cook about 20 minutes. Stir in butter after removing from stove. Dressing may be served plain, or folded into whipped cream for fruit salad topping.

Concentrated Flavor for Salads

1 garlic head, several onions put through food chopper, salt to taste. Cover with vinegar, and let stand in this infusion for 15 days. Squeeze through a piece of cheesecloth and keep in very tight jar. Use a small amount of this with salad oil.

Sandwiches, Canapes and Party Frills

We are always served first to people of note
To please their palate and tickle their throat;
With sweet and dill pickles — some call us
  Hors-d'oeuvres,
We make a nice snack and won't increase your
  curves.

Sandwiches

Pineapple Spears: Slice fresh bread thinly and remove all crusts. Spread each slice with soft butter and a layer of Philadelphia cheese. Sprinkle over this some finely chopped red cherries. Lay a pineapple spear on each slice of bread. Roll up like jelly roll and use toothpick to hold together. One slice of bread will make four sandwiches. Chill in wax paper or damp towel until serving time.

Asparagus Spears: Use firm asparagus tips instead of pineapple spears.

Rolled Sandwiches: Prepare bread as for Spears. Spread with a filling made of: Chopped firm lettuce hearts, green sweet peppers, some pimiento, peeled cucumber, salt, pepper and mayonnaise. Chill and cut when ready to serve. A tiny sprig of parsley or watercress may be tucked in each end.

Date Sandwiches: Cook pitted dates and a little water to a pulp. Cool, and mix with an equal portion of white cream cheese and a little lemon juice. Spread between layers of thinly sliced, buttered nut bread.

Egg Sandwiches: Spread buttered bread with a mixture of coarsely chopped hard cooked egg, finely chopped onion or chives, a bit of curry powder, salt to taste and just enough mayonnaise to moisten. (Try a little garlic salt).

Peanut Butter Sandwiches: Spread bread with peanut butter and cover with sliced banana, or add mashed banana to peanut butter. A layer of peanut butter and a layer of strawberry jam is always acceptable, or, mix some cream cheese with the peanut butter. Try mixing 1 cup peanut butter with ¼ cup mayonnaise and put over this a layer of thinly sliced onion.

Chicken Liver Sandwiches: 1 cup cooked chicken livers (mashed), 2 tbsps. crisp bacon, salt and pepper to taste, 1 tbsp. lemon juice, 2 stalks minced celery and a few drops of Tabasco sauce.

Chicken Salad Sandwiches: Chop cold cooked chicken. Add finely diced celery. Season to taste with salt, pepper, and seasoned salt. Moisten with mayonnaise.

Lobster Sandwiches: Remove cooked lobster meat from shell, and chop. Season with salt and lemon juice. Finely chopped celery may be added. Moisten with mayonnaise.

Ribbon Sandwiches: Build up four slices of bread, alternating white or brown with three layers of effective fillings which blend in color and flavor. To serve, cut down in ½-inch slices; cut each slice in fingers to show all the fillings. These and other sandwiches may be made in advance, wrapped in a damp cloth or wax paper and kept in refrigerator until ready to serve.

Tuna Sandwiches: Combine 1 cup shredded tuna, ½ cup chopped cucumber, 1 tbsp. grated onion, 2 tsps. lemon juice, ¼ cup chopped green pepper, ½ cup chopped celery, salt, pepper and paprika to taste. Moisten with ¼ cup mayonnaise. Spread on bread buttered with Lemon Butter.

Lemon Butter: Cream ½ cup butter; add rind of lemon, 1½ tbsps. lemon juice and 1 tbsp. grated onion.

Tuna, flaked and mixed with parsley, lemon juice and seasoning, and thin slices of onion that have been soaked in a little salted water for half an hour, makes a welcome spread. Substitute salmon or any other preferred fish.

Toasted Sandwiches: Butter fresh bread, add a slice of juicy sweet onion and a slice of back bacon. Grill until bacon is cooked. Add a thin slice of cheese and grill 5 minutes more.

Toast bread slightly and butter it. Spread on it a layer of prepared mustard, layer of sliced cheese, sliced tomato and bacon. Grill until brown.

Another tasty sandwich spread is made by adding bits of cooked lobster or shrimp to 1 can mushroom soup. Grill until nicely set. This spread, with the addition of peas, is delicious served in Butter Cups or Bread Baskets.

Open Face Sandwiches: Remove crust from a slice of bread. Cut in fancy shapes. Spread each slice with softened butter and top with desired filling. Decorate.

Hot Roast Beef Sandwich: Reheat leftover slices of beef. Put on slice of bread (may be toasted on the outside). Season with salt and pepper, and a little horseradish mustard, if desired. Top with another slice of bread and pour hot gravy over sandwich. Serve at once.

Canapes

Toast bread rounds or squares in oven. With pastry decorator force cream cheese through and make an edging on toast cut-outs. Fill center with tart jelly, preferably crabapple or grape.

Spread slices of bread, lightly toasted, with a mixture of cooked lobster meat, some chopped green pepper, dash of curry powder, parsley and enough cream sauce to make right consistency. Sprinkle with grated cheese and buttered bread crumbs. Heat under broiler, 400 degrees. Crab and tuna fish are nice variants.

Spread slices of bread with seasoned butter, and a layer of soft cheese. Cut in small pieces, and on top place bits of uncooked bacon. Put into hot oven or under broiler, until nicely browned.

Combine cream cheese with chopped chives or parsley; spread on buttered toast rounds or squares, and top with whole shrimp.

Spread edges of bread rounds with softened butter; roll in chopped parsley. Spread top with chicken, tuna, or any desired mixture.

A colorful and tasty topping is made by mixing cream cheese with finely chopped peppers and grated carrot.

Seasoned Butter: Make seasoned butters for canapes by creaming butter with any of the following: Mustard, horseradish, lemon juice, onion juice, crushed garlic or garlic salt, parsley.

Party Frills

Spread lettuce leaves with a mixture of creamed cheese, chopped chives, a few chopped nuts, and salt to taste. Place a strip of pimiento across leaf at beginning of roll. Roll up, beginning at core end. Place rolls on a plate and chill for 2 hours or longer. Cut in 1-inch pieces crosswise, and decorate salad plate with these.

Stuff prunes, dates, figs, apricots with cream cheese.

Stuff cut pitted dates or prunes with orange icing or fondant mixture. Top with cherry or a walnut half.

Make cheese balls by working into a paste equal parts of Roquefort and cream cheese, ½ tsp. Worcestershire sauce, ½ tsp. paprika, few grains cayenne. Roll in dessicated coconut, and dip in red sugar or paprika. Top each with a sprig of parsley.

Roll balls or pyramids of cream cheese in chopped nuts, coconut or minced parsley.

Serve radish roses, carrot curls or carrot sticks.

Make celery curls or stuff celery with cream cheese and sprinkle lightly with paprika. To vary, combine cream cheese with grated carrot and a little mayonnaise.

Put on Ritz a colored marshmallow and center with half a cherry. Bake in moderate oven.

Scoop out Tiny Tim tomatoes; fill with chicken salad or cream cheese and top with tiny sprig of parsley.

Roll pineapple spears or chunks in softened cream cheese, then in finely chopped mint leaves.

Using large grapes, cut in half and carefully remove seeds. Chill plain white cream cheese, cut in tiny squares, and put a square between each pair of grape halves. Fasten with cocktail pick.

Spread banana halves with mayonnaise, and roll in grated carrot.

Using a small round scoop, put a small ball of lime or lemon sherbet on top of a tall glass of ginger ale. As a variant, flavor sherbet with a little mint. Add some green food coloring and serve with a tiny mint leaf beside sherbet ball.

Hot Morsel: Remove crusts from slices of very fresh bread. Butter, spread with any savory spread or grated nippy cheese. Add a small asparagus tip and roll up closely. Wrap around it a short piece of thinly sliced bacon. Fasten with toothpick and toast in hot oven.

Dip for Chips or Ritzies: To 1 8-oz. package Philadelphia cheese add 1-2 oz. tin anchovies, plus the oil; beat well together. Add the tiniest crushed clove of garlic, 1 thin slice minced onion (scraped), 2 tsps. prepared horseradish, ½ cup whipped cream. Cream all together. This may be stored in refrigerator before using, and will keep well for a week, if kept in a tightly covered dish. This is an excellent topping for melba toast. Do not butter toast.

Salami Cornucopias (Hors d'Oeuvre)

Slice salami paper thin and cut each slice in half. Twist the half slices into cornucopia shapes. Fill a pastry bag fitted with a small tube with cream cheese, seasoned to taste with horseradish, and force the cheese into the cornucopias. Chill before serving.

Party Cheese Ball

1 lb. sharp cheddar cheese	1 tsp. lemon juice
½ cup pecan nuts	2 tbsps. Tobasco sauce
1 small onion, chopped	2 tbsps. margarine
½ green pepper, chopped	1 8-oz. pkg. cream cheese
½ cup chopped parsley	½ cup Kraft Mayonnaise
1 cup chili sauce	
1 tbsp. Worcestershire sauce	

Grind together the first five ingredients. Mix in remaining ingredients and mould into ball. Chill until firm and frost with the softened cream cheese which has been mixed with margarine. Decorate by rolling ball in chopped parsley, pecans or toasted slivered almonds.

Stuffed Eggs

Cut hard-cooked eggs in half, lengthwise, and remove the yolks. Press the yolks through a sieve and mix them with an equal amount of mayonnaise, some finely chopped chives and parsley, a little curry powder (⅛ tsp.), and salt to taste. Fill the egg whites with the yolk mixture and arrange them in a serving dish. Garnish with mayonnaise and sprinkle with paprika.

Dip For Cheese Board

2 pkgs. cream cheese
2 pkgs. anchovies, straight or
curled
minced clove of garlic
2 tbsps. minced onion

2 tbsps. horseradish
1 tsp. garlic powder
1 tsp. salt
1 cup whipping cream

Mash cheese and anchovies, including the oil, with a fork. Add remaining ingredients, except the cream, and mix well. Whip cream and spoon the mixture into it. Keep in refrigerator in covered bowl. When ready to serve sprinkle finely chopped chives or parsley on top.

Shrimp Butter

1 8-oz. pkg. cream cheese at
room temperature
1 stick margarine
1 tbsp. mayonnaise

1 4½ oz. can cocktail shrimp,
drained
1 pinch garlic powder and onion
flakes
1 tsp. lemon juice

Mix all ingredients well and chill. Delicious with raw vegetables or crackers.

Chicken Liver Paté

1 cup butter
1 lb. chicken livers
1 medium onion, sliced
½ tsp. curry powder

½ tsp. paprika
¼ tsp. salt
⅛ tsp. pepper
garlic powder to taste

Melt butter in saucepan. Cook chicken livers, onion, and seasonings in small amounts until mixture is smooth. Pour into a 9 × 5 inch loaf pan, cover with foil, and refrigerate for 8 hours or longer.

Salmon Paté

1 small tin salmon
1 8-oz. pkg. cream cheese

1 tbsp. lemon juice
¼ cup mayonnaise

Drain, bone, and remove skins from salmon. Mix with remaining ingredients. Shape in log and roll in finely crushed crumbs or minced fresh parsley.

3. Busy Day Meals

Supper Dishes

When at the close of day
Homeward we wend our way,
Our troubles, problems, unfilled wishes
Disappear at the sight of the supper dishes.

Chicken Loaf

⅔ cup chicken stock
4 tbsps. butter
½ cup stale bread crumbs
1 tbsp. pimiento

4 eggs, beaten
2½ cups diced chicken
1 tbsp. finely chopped parsley
Salt and pepper to taste

Melt butter; stir in crumbs and brown. Remove from fire and add remaining ingredients. Turn into a greased loaf pan and bake slowly in pan of water at 350 degrees for 1 hour. Serves 8 to 10 people.

Meat Loaf

1½ lbs. ground round steak
1 lb. ground lean pork or veal
1 egg, unbeaten
1 small tin tomato soup
1 cup milk

½ cup bread or cracker crumbs
1 tsp. salt
¼ tsp. pepper
1 medium-sized onion, minced

Pack mixture in loaf pan and place slices of bacon on top. Bake for 1 hour in oven 350 degrees.

For a nice variation, mix 2 tbsps. brown sugar, 4 tbsps. ketchup, ¼ tsp. nutmeg and 1 tsp. dry mustard. Pour over top instead of bacon.

Ham Loaf

1 lb. ground ham	1 cup milk
1 lb. ground lean pork	1 small onion, minced
1 cup bread crumbs or 2 cups	¼ tsp. pepper
crushed cornflakes	1 tbsp. minced parlsey
2 eggs, beaten	

Combine all ingredients. Form into loaf and bake for 1 hour at 350 degrees.

Variation: About 20 minutes before cooking time is up, make a paste of the following ingredients and baste frequently: ⅓ cup brown sugar, 1 tsp. prepared mustard, ¼ tsp. cinnamon, 1 tsp. vinegar, 1 tbsp. water.

Veal Loaf

2 lbs. veal	1 cup cracker crumbs
¼ lb. salt pork	1 cup stock or water
1½ tsps. salt	1 egg, unbeaten
1 small green pepper	½ tsp. sage or marjoram
1 large onion, chopped	2 tbsps. butter
	1 tbsp. lemon juice

Chop veal and pork very fine. Add onion, seeded and chopped pepper, crumbs, lemon juice, one-half the stock, egg and seasoning. Mix together well. Pack in greased loaf pan and cook in oven 350 degrees for about 2½ hours, basting occasionally with the butter and remaining stock or water.

Liver Loaf

1 lb. beef liver	½ cup stock
½ lb. pork sausage	1 tbsp. lemon juice
1 onion, chopped	1 tsp. salt
2 eggs, beaten	⅛ tsp. pepper
1 cup dry bread crumbs	1 tsp. celery salt
1 tsp. Worcestershire sauce	Bacon slices

Cover liver with hot water; drain, after it has simmered for 5 minutes. Reserve liquid for stock. Put liver and onion through food chopper, using medium blade. Add remaining ingredients, except bacon. Form into loaf in a 5½ × 10½-inch pan. Top with bacon slices and bake in oven 350 degrees for about 45 minutes.

Lasagna

1 pkg. Lasagna, cooked and drained
1 lb. ground beef
1 medium onion, minced
1 or 2 cloves garlic, minced
2 tbsps. olive or cooking oil
1 8-oz. can tomato sauce
1 5½ oz. can tomato paste

1 10-oz. can mushrooms or sliced fresh mushrooms
2 tsps. salt
¾ cup cold water
1 tsp. oregano
1½ cups creamed cottage cheese
1 6-oz. pkg. sliced Mozzarella cheese

Cook lasagna according to instructions on package. Sauté onion and garlic in oil. Add ground beef and brown, breaking it apart with a fork. Stir in mushrooms with liquid, tomato paste, tomato sauce, salt, oregano, water, and simmer for about 15 mins.

Spread ⅓ of meat mixture in a 9 × 13 inch baking dish. Cover with ⅓ lasagna. Alternate another ⅓ of sauce and lasagna. Cover with cottage cheese, Parmesan cheese and a little of the meat sauce. Cover with remaining lasagna and sauce. Arrange Mozzarella cheese slices on top and bake at 350° for 20 to 30 minutes.

Chili

1 lb. ground beef
1 can kidney beans
1 tin tomato soup
⅔ cup water
1 medium onion, chopped
1 tbsp. cooking oil

1 tsp. salt
2 or 3 tsps. chili powder
1 garlic clove, crushed
1 tsp. vinegar
½ tsp. Italian seasoning

Heat oil in large skillet. Add the ground beef, onion, garlic and saute until lightly browned, stirring frequently. Add remaining ingredients and simmer about ½ hour, stirring occasionally. Serve over rice, if desired, or rice may be added to the sauce. ½ cup chopped green pepper may be added and the amount of chili powder, according to taste.

Pizza

1 pkg. dry yeast	1½ tsps. sugar
4½ cups all-purpose flour	1 medium onion, minced
(approx.)	1 garlic clove, minced
1½ cups water	1 tsp. herb seasoning
salt	¼ tsp. hot red pepper, crushed
olive or salad oil	1 16-oz. pkg. Mozzarella cheese,
1 16-oz. can tomatoes	shredded
1 6-oz. can tomato paste	

In large bowl, combine yeast, 2 cups flour and ½ tsp. salt. In small saucepan, heat water until warm (130F).

With mixer at low speed, gradually beat water into dry ingredients until just blended. Increase speed to medium; beat 2 minutes, scraping bowl occasionally. Beat in ½ cup flour to make a thick batter and continue to beat for 2 more minutes, scraping bowl often. With spoon, stir in additional flour (about 1½ cups) to make a soft dough.

Turn dough onto floured canvas, kneading until smooth and elastic. If needed, add a little more flour. Shape dough into ball; place in greased large bowl and grease top of dough. Cover and let rise, in warm place, until doubled in bulk.

Prepare sauce as follows: In large saucepan cook onion and garlic in 1 tbsp. hot oil until tender. Add tomatoes with the liquid, tomato paste, sugar, herb seasoning, red pepper and ½ tsp. salt. Bring to boiling point, stirring to break up tomatoes. Reduce heat to low, cover partially, and simmer 20 minutes. Cool.

Punch dough down and cut in half. Turn onto lightly floured canvas. Cover and let rise for about 15 minutes.

Preheat oven to 450. Grease 2 12-inch pizza pans. Roll each dough half into 13-inch circles. Place in prepared pans, pinching up edges to form a rim; brush with oil.

Sprinkle circles with ½ the cheese, top with tomato sauce and sprinkle with remaining cheese. Bake 20 minutes or until crusts are golden. Before sprinkling top with cheese you may add any favorite topping as sliced mushrooms, red and green peppers cut in desired shapes, sliced pepperoni, sliced olives, etc. Cut each circle in 8 wedges.

Spaghetti Sauce

2 tbsps. bacon drippings or margarine
1 cup diced onion
1 cup chopped celery
1 cup chopped green pepper
1 lb. ground beef
2 tsps. salt
½ tsp. pepper
¼ tsp. thyme
1 tsp. garlic salt
2 bay leaves
½ cup tomato paste
2 cups tomato juice
1 tin mushrooms

Brown onions, celery and green pepper in margarine. Add meat and fry until brown. Add remaining ingredients and cook on low heat for 1 hour or longer. Serve on spaghetti, topped with Parmesan cheese.

Chop Suey

3 cups cooked spaghetti
3 onions
1 lb. ground beef
⅓ bacon fat
1 large tin tomatoes
2 tbsps. sugar
2 tsps. salt
¼ tsp. pepper
½ lb. mushrooms
1 cup finely chopped celery (optional)

Heat fat; add chopped onions, beef, celery and mushrooms. Saute for about 10 minutes or until beef loses its color, stirring occasionally. Put these ingredients and the spaghetti into a large casserole. Add tomatoes and seasoning. Stir well. Bake in oven 400 degrees about 45 minutes. Stir occasionally.

Baked Bean Loaf

1½ cups baked beans
¼ cup finely chopped green pepper
1 cup soft bread crumbs
1 egg, unbeaten
¼ cup finely chopped onion
½ cup canned tomatoes
1 cup minced ham
1 tsp. salt
¼ tsp. pepper

Put the beans through a sieve or mash with a fork. Simmer the onion and pepper in the tomatoes for 15 minutes. Mix the mashed beans with this mixture. Add the remaining ingredients. Shape into loaf in greased pan and sprinkle the top lightly with flour and paprika. Bake at 350 degrees for about 30 minutes.

Salmon Loaf

2 cups salmon, flaked
2 cups soft bread crumbs
¾ cup milk
2 eggs, beaten
⅛ tsp. pepper

1 tsp. salt
1 tbsp. minced onion
2 tsps. lemon juice
½ cup chopped celery (optional)

Remove skin from fresh or canned fish. Mix all ingredients and place in a greased loaf pan, dot with butter and bake at 350 degrees for about 45 minutes. Serves 8.

Sauce for Salmon Loaf: Melt ¼ cup butter in double boiler; stir in 2 tbsps. flour. Gradually add ¾ cup milk, ½ tsp. salt, dash of pepper and cook until it thickens. Remove from fire and stir in ¼ cup lemon juice, some grated rind and 2 egg yolks. Reheat but do not boil.

Salmon-Spaghetti Loaf

2 cups soft bread crumbs
1 cup cooked spaghetti
1 cup milk
2 egg yolks, beaten
2 cups salmon

1 tsp. salt
¼ cup melted butter
¼ cup rich milk or cream
Pepper and paprika to taste
2 egg whites, beaten

Heat the milk and bread crumbs; add to beaten egg yolks and blend well. Add all other ingredients except the egg whites. Cool mixture and fold in the stiffly beaten egg whites. Form into loaf and bake for 1 hour at 350 degrees.

Ham Buffet Ring

1 can tomato soup
¾ cup water
2 tbsps. gelatin
½ cup cold water
3-oz. pkg. cream cheese
2 tbsps. lemon juice

1 tbsp. grated onion
½ cup mayonnaise
1 tsp. prepared mustard
1 tsp. sugar
2 cups ground cooked ham

Combine soup and water; heat thoroughly. Remove from heat, add gelatin which has been softened in the ½ cup water. Add cheese; beat smooth with beater. Cool. Add lemon juice, onion, mayonnaise, mustard, sugar, and ham. Rinse a ring mould (8½-inch) with cold water; pour in mixture and chill. Unmold on salad greens and garnish with hard boiled eggs and olives. Makes 8 to 10 servings. May be put in individual moulds. This is nice served with French Fried potatoes or Potato Chips.

Baked Beans

1 lb. yellow eye beans	⅓ cup molasses
½ lb. salt pork	1 tsp. dry mustard
4 tbsps. sugar	2 tsps. salt
1 small onion	¼ tsp. pepper

Soak beans overnight. In the morning, add to beans ½ tsp. soda, and boil for 10 minutes. Then run cold water through the beans in a strainer. Dice pork in small pieces. Place half of pork in bottom of bean pot with onion. Put beans into pot and put the rest of the pork on top. Mix the other ingredients with some water and add enough hot water to come to the level of the beans. Bake in oven 300 degrees for 6 hours or longer, adding water occasionally but not enough to flood beans.

Corned Beef Hash

Take equal amounts of chopped or canned corn beef and chopped cooked potatoes, 1 finely chopped onion, pepper to taste, and extra salt, if needed. Sauté the onion in 4 tbsps. melted fat. Add chopped meat, potatoes, pepper, and brown. Hash may be stirred while browning, or browned nicely on one side and folded over like an omelet, and served on a platter. Any leftover meat may be substituted for the corned beef.

Meat and Rice Curry

1 lb. or less cold beef or chicken	1 tbsp. curry powder
3 tbsps. butter	1 cup stock or canned tomatoes
1 onion, chopped	Salt and lemon juice to taste
1 small green pepper, chopped	Cooked rice

Melt butter, add curry, onion, pepper, and fry until golden brown. Add cubed meat and cook for 5 minutes longer. Add stock or tomatoes and cook slowly for one-half hour, stirring well. Lastly, add salt and lemon juice, and serve hot on cooked rice.

Macaroni and Cheese

Boil 2 cups macaroni in salted water and drain well. Put into double boiler about 4 tbsps. minced onion, 2 tbsps. butter and stir in 1 tbsp. flour, ¼ tsp. dry mustard, ¾ tsp. salt, ⅛ tsp. pepper. Add slowly 2 cups milk and cook until smooth. To this add three-quarters of the cheese used, allowing about ½ lb. grated cheese for this amount, and let stand until melted. Put macaroni into baking dish and pour the cheese sauce over it. Cover with remaining cheese and buttered bread crumbs. Bake in oven 350 degrees for about 30 minutes.

Tomato-Macaroni Supper Dish

1 cup uncooked macaroni	2 tsps. salt
¾ cup chopped onion	¼ tsp. pepper
½ cup chopped green pepper	¼ tsp. paprika
2 tbsps. butter or bacon fat	¼ tsp. dry mustard
½ lb. ground beef	½ tsp. Worcestershire sauce
1 cup whole kernel corn	2 cups tomato juice
	1 cup (sharp) grated cheese

Cook macaroni in boiling water, until tender; drain. Meanwhile, cook onion and green pepper in butter until tender. Add ground beef and brown well. Blend in flour and seasonings. Stir in tomato juice. Cook, stirring constantly, until thick and smooth. Combine macaroni with meat, sauce, and corn. Sprinkle grated cheese on top. Bake in casserole at 350 degrees for 1 hour.

Broccoli Casserole

1 pkg. frozen broccoli (fresh preferred) cooked and drained	1 tsp. curry powder
	1 tbsp. lemon juice
	¼ tsp. black pepper
1 can tuna, drained and flaked	1 tsp. chopped pimiento
1 can mushroom soup	(optional)
½ cup or more mayonnaise	

Put broccoli into greased casserole and cover with tuna. Combine remaining ingredients and pour over tuna. Sprinkle with buttered bread crumbs, and bake in oven 350 degrees until bubbly and brown. Serve hot.

Beef and Cabbage Casserole

4 strips bacon, finely diced
1 cup finely diced onion
1 lb. lean ground beef
1 small head green cabbage,
    shredded
1 small can tomato soup,
    undiluted
1 tsp. salt
¼ tsp. pepper
1 tsp. all-purpose seasoning
½ cup soft bread crumbs
1 cup beef bouillon
1 cup boiling water

Fry bacon until crisp; set aside. Add onion and sauté until it is transparent. Add salt, pepper, seasoning, tomato soup and bread crumbs to meat and mix well. Add and mix well with onion and half the bacon. Place a layer of shredded cabbage in a 1½ quart casserole. Top with a layer of meat mixture. Continue alternating layers, ending with cabbage. Dissolve bouillon cube in 1 cup boiling water and pour over the top. Sprinkle top with remaining bacon. Cover and bake at 350° for 1 hour. Remove cover during last fifteen minutes to brown cabbage.

Hamburgers

1 lb. ground meat
1 tsp. (scant) salt
⅛ tsp. pepper
⅛ tsp. paprika
1 medium-sized onion,
    chopped
½ cup soft bread crumbs or
    ¼ cup evaporated milk
Minced parsley (optional)
Worcestershire sauce (optional)

Mix all together and shape into flat cakes. Fry in well greased pan until nicely browned on both sides.

Hamburger Fluffs

1 lb. ground beef
2 tbsps. flour
½ tsp. Worcestershire sauce
½ tsp. pepper
1 tsp. salt
1 small onion, minced
Pinch thyme
Pinch marjoram
¾ cup undiluted evaporated milk
¾ cup water

Put beef into large bowl; add all ingredients except milk and water. Whip mixture with large spoon or electric mixer. Add milk and water slowly, beating constantly. When all liquid has been absorbed, cover bowl and let stand in refrigerator for a few hours. (Mixture may be cooked at once, but texture improves on standing). Drop in mounds, about 16, on hot greased griddle. Brown on each side.

Hamburger Balls

Make little balls of hamburger mixture. Drop in rapidly boiling salted water. Meat is cooked sufficiently when balls rise to the top. Drain, put on platter and pour over balls nicely browned onions.

Hamburger Casserole

1½ lbs. ground beef	25 Ritz crackers, coarsely crushed
1 onion, chopped	1 20-oz. tin tomatoes
½ green pepper, chopped	¼ tsp. ground black pepper
1 tsp. salt	¼ tsp. oregano
1 6-oz. tin tomato paste	Pinch of basil and thyme

Brown beef, stirring lightly to break it up. Drain off excess fat. Add onion and green pepper. Stir until lightly cooked. Add tomato paste, tomatoes and tomato liquid, reserving some tomatoes for garnishing. Put in buttered casserole (½ qt. size). Top with Ritz cracker crumbs. Bake at 375 degrees for 25 minutes. Remove from oven and garnish with green pepper rings and reserved tomatoes. Return to oven for about 5-10 minutes.

Frankfurters

1 lb. frankfurters	¾ cup ketchup
2 tbsps. flour	3 tbsps. vinegar
3 tbsps. water	1 tbsp. sugar
1 cup water	1 tsp. prepared mustard

Cut frankfurters in halves, lengthwise. Put into deep covered skillet. Mix the flour and water, add remaining ingredients and pour this sauce over frankfurters. Cover and bring to the boiling point. Decrease heat and simmer for about 20 minutes. Serve with the sauce. Nice with fluffy mashed potatoes.

Clam Whiffle Casserole

12 soda crackers	1 tbsp. chopped green pepper
1 cup milk	¼ tsp. Worcestershire sauce
¼ cup melted butter	dash of salt, pepper
1 can clams, minced	2 eggs, beaten
2 tbsps. chopped onion	

Soak the crumbled crackers in the milk for a few minutes. Then add other ingredients, eggs last. Pour into a greased casserole and bake in a 350 degree oven for forty-five minutes, uncovered, 3 to 4 servings.

Corn Casserole

2½ cups canned corn, cream
    style
1 cup milk
4 cups cubed cooked potatoes

4 hard boiled eggs, sliced
½ cup cracker crumbs
Salt, pepper and paprika to taste

Mix corn and milk together. Arrange potatoes, eggs and corn in layers in greased baking dish. Season each layer with the salt, pepper and paprika. Bake at 400 degrees about 20 minutes.

Cheese Souffle No. 1

1 cup grated cheese
2 eggs, beaten
½ tsp. salt

2 or 3 pieces buttered bread, cut
    in pieces
2 cups milk
Bacon

Put bread and cheese, in layers, into a greased casserole. Combine beaten eggs, milk and salt. Pour over bread and cheese. Cut strips of bacon in pieces and place over top. Bake in moderate oven for about 40-45 minutes.

Cheese Souffle No.2

To 1 cup Medium White Sauce add ¾ cup (or less) grated cheese. When cheese is melted add the beaten yolks of 3 eggs, ¼ tsp. salt, a little paprika or cayenne. Cook these ingredients until mixture thickens, and then cool. Fold in the stiffly beaten egg whites and bake in an ungreased baking dish in oven 325 degrees until firm, about 40-45 minutes.

Fluffy Omelet

4 eggs, separated   6 tbsps. hot water
2 egg yolks   1 tbsp. butter
½ tsp. salt

Beat the 6 egg yolks until thick and lemon colored. Beat whites quite stiff. Add water and salt to yolks, mix thoroughly and fold the whites into the yolk mixture. Have butter heated in frying pan and pour in the mixture immediately. Let stand over moderate heat for about 2 minutes, then place in hot oven and cook until set. Remove from oven and make a deep crease across omelet. Tip the pan and with egg turner or spatula, life around edges carefully until you can fold in half without breaking. Serve at once.

Note: To make an omelet fluffier, and of better texture, the number of egg yolks should exceed the whites.

Cheese Omelet

Follow preceding recipe, only before folding over, spread omelet with grated cheese. Finely minced bacon or ham may be used in place of the cheese. The addition of chopped chives, parsley, or seasoned salt is good.

For a Sweet Omelet add 1 tbsp. sugar to yolk mixture and spread with jam, jelly, or sweetened fruit.

Spanish Meat Balls

1 lb. ground veal   1 tsp. salt
1 cup bread crumbs   1 egg, beaten
1 tbsp. chopped onion   1 small can cream of tomato
1 tbsp. chopped green pepper   soup
                               1 bouillon cube
                               1 cup water

Mix veal, crumbs, onion, pepper, salt and egg and form into small balls; brown on both sides in butter. Dissolve bouillon cube in water, add soup and bring to the boiling point. Pour this over the meat balls and simmer slowly for 30 minutes. Thicken gravy with a little flour and serve on platter with boiled rice.

Cottage Pie

2 cups diced leftover meat   3 tbsps. flour
    (lamb, beef, pork or veal)   1 can vegetable soup
2 tbsps. butter   Mashed potatoes

Melt butter in frying pan and brown the meat in it. Sprinkle the flour over the meat and blend well. Add soup and stir until thick and boiling. Pour into a baking dish or casserole and cover with a layer of leftover mashed potato that has been made fluffy again by beating up with a small amount of hot milk. Place in a moderate oven 375 degrees to brown, about 15 minutes.

Potato Casserole

1½ lbs. potatoes   **Sauce:**
4 or 5 tbsps. grated cheese   1 tbsp. butter
Bread crumbs   1½ tbsps. flour
1 tbsp. butter   Finely cut onions
    Water or vegetable stock
    Salt to taste

Peel and slice freshly boiled potatoes. Put a layer into greased casserole. Pour some of the sauce over the potatoes. Alternate layers. Spread over this the grated cheese. Top with bread crumbs and the 1 tbsp. butter. Put into oven 375 degrees until heated through and browned on top.

Easy Supper Dishes

Line dishes, sides and bottoms, with mashed potatoes, about ¼ inch in thickness. Fill centres with any of the following:

Chicken Filling: Cut up cooked chicken in small pieces. Add chopped celery, onions, peas or any desired vegetable. Add enough medium white sauce to mix ingredients to right consistency. Fill centre of dish and bake at 350 for about ½ hour or until a delicate brown.

Ham Filling: Mince ham quite fine and add a little prepared mustard, salt and pepper to taste. A little chopped or crushed pineapple improves the flavor. Fill lined pan and bake, as directed.

Meat Filling: Use ground beef. Add salt, pepper and enough undiluted tomato soup to mix. Onion or your favorite seasoning may be used. Fill lined pan and bake, as directed.

Râpe Pie (Tarte á la Rappure)

This traditional Acadian dish may be made with clams, venison, duck or rabbit, as well as the more usual pork and chicken. In Acadian homes there is a large (oven-sized) pan for this dish, which keeps well for several meals. It can be made for a small family in this manner: You will need a baking pan with 4-5 inch sides, enough potatoes to fill the pan twice, 3-5 onions (depending on how much you like them), ¼ lb. clear salt pork, 1 chicken, and 2 lbs. of fresh lean pork for each 7-10 lbs. of potatoes, a strong grater, a jelly bag, ½ lb. shortening, salt and pepper, boiling water.

Method: In a large pot boil the meats together with some chopped onion, until the chicken almost leaves the bones. While this is cooking peel and grate the potatoes. Place the grated potatoes in a jelly bag and squeeze them as dry as possible. Measure the water squeezed from the potatoes before throwing it away. Put the potatoes (covered tightly) in the refrigerator, until the meat is cooked. (The potatoes may be prepared the night before. If there is any discoloration, scrape this off before continuing). Now, take the meat from the pot. Remove bones and break meat into serving-size pieces. Bring the stock to a strong boil. Put the grated potatoes in a very large bowl or pan and add the hot stock, equal to the water that has been removed from the potatoes. This should be added gradually and stirred thoroughly after each addition This stirring is as important to the success of the Rape Pie as it was in making old-fashioned laundry starch. The potatoes should become quite clear and similar to thick starch. When it is well stirred pour half of this mixture into the baking pan in which shortening has been melted, to a depth of about ¼ inch. Work it well into the corners. Cover with all the meat and 1-2 of the chopped onions. Add the rest of the potato mixture and sprinkle the top with finely chopped salt pork. Bake in a hot oven 425 degrees for several hours until a nice brown crust forms all around it. From time to time baste the top with some of the shortening from the sides or add some hot water or stock if it seems to be drying out.

The fragrance of this dish while cooking makes waiting almost unendurable! An especial favorite during the hunting season and following Mass on Christmas Eve.

Leftovers

Now, with my leftovers, what shall I do?
Why, make a dish that's enticing and new.

Mcat Biscuit Roll

4 cups flour
6 tsps. baking powder
2 tsps. salt
2 cups shortening
1 cup milk

3 cups ground cooked meat
1 tbsp. minced onion
1 cup rich gravy or tomato puree
1 tsp. marjoram or favorite herbs

Make the biscuit dough and roll out in an oblong shape. Spread the dough with above mixture and roll up, like jelly roll. Bake in moderate oven 375 degrees. Cut in 2-inch wide slices and serve with Tomato and Mushroom Sauce.

Note: Any kind of cooked minced meat with the addition of some minced onion, chopped cooked vegetables, seasoning and some thick cold gravy may be used in the same way.

Meat Pie

2 cups cubed meat
½ cup chopped onion
½ cup chopped celery
½ cup chopped green pepper

1 cup cubed vegetables
1 can peas
1 cup gravy (more or less)
Coarse bread crumbs

Brown celery, onions and green pepper in a little hot fat; add to combined meat and vegetables (potatoes and carrots). Add peas. Add gravy and seasoning to taste. Put into casserole, top with bread crumbs browned in butter. Bake in oven 375 degrees for about 40-45 minutes.

Appetizing Shortcakes

Make Hot Biscuits: Split, butter, and put beween biscuits any of the following fillings:

Salmon Filling: Blend 1 can cream of celery soup with ⅓ cup milk. Add 1 cup drained flaked salmon (fresh or canned), 1 cup drained cooked peas and some seasoning. Heat thoroughly and serve like shortcakes.

Shrimp and Pea Filling: 4 tbsps. butter, 2 tbsps. flour, ½ tsp. salt, ½ tsp. paprika, 1½ cups milk, 1 cup cooked peas, 1 cup cleaned and cut shrimps. Melt butter, add flour, salt and paprika; stir until blended and smooth. Add milk gradually and cook until thickened, stirring constantly. Add the prepared shrimps and the peas which have been thoroughly drained. Heat through and serve between the layers and on top of biscuits.

Meat and Vegetable Filling: Dice any leftover meat and vegetables. Combine with some finely chopped green pepper, parsley, chives, salt and pepper to taste. Mix to desired consistency with leftover gravy, celery or cream of mushroom soup. Heat and serve shortcake style.

Fish Filling: Use the same ingredients as for meat filling but mix with Medium White Sauce.

Lobster or Crab Filling: Melt 2 tbsps. butter in saucepan. Blend in 2 tbsps. flour ¼ tsp. salt and ⅛ tsp. pepper. Add 1 can Tomato sauce, 1 scant cup grated nippy cheese, and 1 egg slightly beaten. When cheese is melted, stir in ¾ cup milk and cook for 2 or 3 minutes. Just before serving add flaked lobster or crab meat. Serve as shortcakes, or, in Bread Baskets or patty shells.

Note: In making creamed dishes, use the same proportions of sauce and solid food. Add meat or whatever is being used to the creamed sauce, heat thoroughly and use in patty shells, Bread Baskets, serve on toast, or use in making Fish Nests.

Fish Cakes

Mash well leftover fish and potatoes. Add some finely chopped onion, 1 slightly beaten egg, salt, pepper and any other preferred seasoning. Form into patties and fry a golden brown on each side. Serve hot. For a nice change, top each serving with a poached egg.

Hot Potato Salad

Butter casserole or baking dish. Cut up and put into dish 2 cups cold cooked potatoes and 1 chopped onion. Add 1 cup grated cheese, a good sized piece of butter, salt and pepper. Add any scraps of leftover ham, meat or bacon. Bake until cheese is melted.

Potato Pudding

Mash any leftover potatoes, whole or mashed, with some milk, butter, salt. Add any leftover meat diced fine or minced, 1 egg beaten. Put into buttered casserole and bake for ½ hour.

Other uses for Leftovers

Use any leftover meat or fish by adding vegetables and suitable seasonings. Make into a jellied salad or mix with salad dressing and serve on crisp lettuce.

Mix meat or fish with gravy or White Sauce, and serve in heated pastry shells or Toasted Bread Baskets.

Mix meat with cream of asparagus soup (undiluted); add chopped hard boiled eggs, and mix with a little milk or vegetable stock if too thick. Serve hot on toast.

Leftover meats, fish, and vegetables, suitably moistened, and used alone, or combined with rice, crumbs, egg or cream sauce make excellent stuffing for tomatoes, peppers, or baked potato shells. Or, bake mixture in greased custard cups, in pan of hot water. Keep covered while baking. Top with buttered crumbs and brown just before serving.

Mix diced ham, hard boiled eggs, and mushrooms with seasoned White Sauce and serve in Bread Baskets or patty shells.

To use any leftover slices of beef, chicken or turkey, reheat in medium hot oven, by placing between two cookie sheets, having sprinkled meat with water. Serve with hot gravy as an open face sandwich.

Dip cold slices of beef, chicken or turkey in seasoned flour, then in slightly beaten egg, and lastly in fine bread crumbs. Fry for 1 minute, in deep fat. Serve with gravy.

Leftover chicken and turkey carcasses, skin, gravy, bits of dressing, giblets and neck make good soup stock. Cover with cold water and let come to a boil. Simmer for several hours and strain. To the strained stock add finely chopped vegetables, rice or barley (the amount depending on quantity of stock). Add additional seasoning to taste.

Combine diced leftover meat with chopped green pepper, celery, onion, gravy and water. Cook until meat is tender; season and thicken. Good for biscuit shortcake filling or for hot sandwiches.

Spread slices of meat loaf with ketchup and broil slowly for about 10 minutes, then top with grated cheese, and return to broiler until cheese melts.

Cube or slice cold boiled potatoes and put into baking dish. Pour over potatoes a cream or cheese sauce seasoned with grated onion, celery salt, little curry powder. Cover with buttered bread crumbs, and bake until thoroughly heated through.

Roll out pastry and cut in squares. Spread thinly with mustard. Place on each square a frankfurter or sausage and roll up. Bake in hot oven 400 degrees for 12-15 minutes.

Cut stale cake into strips. Pile the strips, one on top of the other, with a whipped cream filling between each one. Press slices together and wrap in wax paper, then in damp towel. Chill thoroughly, unwrap and frost with more of the filling. Garnish attractively with cherries and nuts. Serve in slices. Or, break up any stale cake or cookies and combine with a soft custard to which has been added a little whipped cream. Chill for several hours. Decorate with berries or any desired fruit.

4.   Baked Goods

Bread and Rolls

Some prefer cologne, but give me instead,
The delicious aroma of fresh baking bread.

Green Shutters Brown Bread

1 cup rolled oats
1 shredded wheat biscuit

1 cup each all-bran, grapenuts,
   cornflakes and any leftover
   cooked cereal
¼ cup cornmeal

Scald these ingredients with 3 cups boiling water and add:
½ cup molasses, 2 tbsps. shortening, 1 tbsp. salt

Mix all together and let cool to lukewarm. Add 1 yeast cake which has been dissolved for 5 minutes in a little warm water (¼ cup). Add enough flour (some graham, rye or whole wheat may be used), to make to consistency of white bread. Knead well on floured canvas. Let rise until double in bulk. Shape into loaves and let rise in warm place until light and pans are full. Bake in hot oven 450 degrees for the first 10 minutes, decreasing heat to 300 degrees to complete baking.

Note: This is a favorite bread. I have given the approximate ingredients, but each baking varies, depending on the dry cereal and the kind of leftover cooked cereal on hand. I find that kneading improves this bread and the quantity of flour required depends on your good judgement and sense of touch.

Whole Wheat Bread

2 cups unsifted whole wheat flour	4 cups sifted white flour
	1 tsp. salt

Measure into large mixing bowl 2½ cups warm (not hot) water. Add 2 pkgs. dry yeast. Add ½ the flour mixture, ¼ cup soft shortening, ¼ cup honey or brown sugar. Beat on medium speed for 2 minutes. Add remaining flour mixture and blend in with rubber spatula. Cover with waxed paper and let rise in warm place until double in bulk. Stir down batter by beating or kneading 25 strokes. Divide batter into 2 greased 9x5x3 loaf pans. Let rise until pans are full and bake in 350° oven for about 40 minutes.

White Bread

10 cups all-purpose flour	3 tbsps. sugar
1 yeast cake or 2 pkgs. dry yeast	2 tbsps. shortening, melted
1½ tbsps. salt	4 cups luke warm water, more if needed

Sieve flour and salt in a large mixing bowl. Make well in centre. Add water, yeast, and shortening. Sprinkle over this the sugar and let stand until the yeast is dissolved and bubbly.

Begin to knead in the flour and continue kneading until dough is light and elastic, adding more flour, if necessary.

Put aside in a warm place until the dough has doubled in bulk; knead again.

Form into loaves and put in greased pans. Let rise until pans are full. Bake for about 1 hour, at 400° for the first 15 minutes, decreasing heat to 350° to finish baking. If desired, brush bread with melted butter when taken from oven.

Sufficient for three medium sized loaves.

Steamed Brown Bread

½ cup flour	2 cups sour milk
1 cup bran flakes	1 tsp. soda
1 cup corn meal	½ tsp. salt
½ cup molasses	

Put dry ingredients into mixing bowl. Dissolve soda in sour milk and add with the molasses to make batter. Pour into greased mold and steam for 3 hours.

Barley Bread

3 cups white flour	½ yeast cake
2 cups barley flour	1 tbsp. sugar
1 dessertspoon salt	

Dissolve yeast cake in a little lukewarm water and add sugar. Add this to flour mixture (do not sift dark flour) with sufficient warm water to make a rather stiff batter. Turn into greased long loaf pan and set in warm place to rise, covering with greased wax paper. When pan is full put into very hot oven 450 degrees and after about 10 minutes decrease heat. Bake slowly for 1 hour.

Hot Cross Buns

1 yeast cake	1 egg
¼ cup lukewarm water	½ tsp. salt
1 cup milk	¾ cup currants
½ cup sugar	½ tsp. cinnamon
3½ cups flour	½ tsp. cloves
¼ cup butter or shortening	1 egg white

Dissolve yeast in lukewarm water. Scald milk, add 1 tbsp. sugar and cool to lukewarm. Add yeast and half the flour. Beat smooth, cover, and let set in warm place to rise for about 1¼ hours. Cream shortening, add remaining sugar and add to sponge. Add well beaten egg, salt, spices, currants, and the remaining flour to make a soft dough, adding a little more flour, if necessary. Mix well. Place in greased bowl, set again in warm place for another hour. Roll out on lightly floured canvas or shape into round buns and place about 2 inches apart on greased baking sheet. Cover lightly and let rise until double in bulk. Glaze with a mixture of egg white and water. With a sharp knife cut a cross in top of each bun. Bake in oven 425 degrees for about 15 minutes. While still warm, fill gashes with white frosting to form a cross.

Plum Loaf

¼ cup shortening
½ cup granulated sugar
1 egg, beaten
1 yeast cake
1 tsp. salt

½ tsp. mace
6 cups flour
1 cup lukewarm water
1 cup scalded milk, cooled
2 cups seeded raisins

Dissolve yeast and 1 tbsp. of the sugar in liquid. Add 2 cups of the flour, the well creamed shortening and sugar and beat until smooth. Let rise in warm place until light. Add raisins, salt, mace, egg, and remainder of flour and knead well. Place in greased bowl and let rise, in warm place, until double in bulk. Mould into loaves and let rise until light. Bake 50-60 minutes in 325 degree oven. Brush with melted butter after removing from pans.

Rolls

5 cups flour
1 tsp. salt
1 cup milk and 1 cup water
    (scalded and cooled)
1 yeast cake

3 tbsps. sugar
4 tbsps. melted butter
2 eggs, beaten

Sift flour and salt into large mixing bowl. Make a well in center and pour in the milk and water which has been cooled to lukewarm. Add yeast cake, sugar and butter; let stand for 5 minutes, until dissolved. Add the slightly beaten eggs and mix well, adding a little extra flour, only if necessary. Cover and let rise in warm place until double in bulk. With buttered fingers, cut pieces of dough and form into rolls. Place in greased muffin tins and brush tops with melted butter. Let rise in warm place until light and bake in hot oven 400 degrees. This recipe makes about 65 rolls.

Cinnamon Rolls: When dough has doubled in bulk, roll out (as for jelly roll) to a rectangular sheet. Spread it generously with white or brown sugar, cinnamon and raisins. Roll up, slice, and place in pan. Let rise and bake in oven 375 degrees. For a nice variant, add some finely chopped peel instead of the raisins.

Parkerhouse Rolls: Roll dough ¼-inch thick. Cut with biscuit cutter and brush with melted butter. Make a deep crease across the middle of each one. Fold over and press edges together lightly. Place rolls close together on greased pan, let rise until light and bake in oven 400 degrees for about 12 minutes.

Clothespin Rolls: Around a long greased clothespin wrap, in a spiral, a narrow strip of the rolled dough, about $\frac{1}{4}$-inch thick and $\frac{1}{2}$-inch wide. Place on greased baking sheet and let rise until dough is double in bulk. Bake, as directed, and as soon as removing from oven, twist clothespins and pull out.

Cheese Sticks: Cut rolled dough in slim strips, about 7 inches long. Brush with melted butter and roll in grated cheese. Place well apart on greased baking sheet, cover, and let rise until light. Bake in moderately hot oven 375 degrees.

Bread Sticks: Cut rolled dough in slim strips, as for Cheese Sticks. Brush strips with water and roll lightly in cornmeal. Place well apart on greased baking sheet. Cover, and let rise until double in bulk. Bake about 10 minutes in oven 375 degrees. Sticks are greatly improved if each one is brushed with melted butter, sprinkled with garlic or onion salt before dipping in the cornmeal.

Croutons: Trim crusts from $\frac{3}{4}$-inch thick slices of bread. Spread liberally with extra salt butter or margarine. Cut in cubes or any desired shapes. Put on ungreased baking sheet and brown in oven 350 degrees. Watch carefully as croutons brown quickly.

Butter Cups or Bread Baskets: Brush thin slices of bread, crusts removed, with melted butter. Press into muffin tins. Toast in oven 350 degrees. Used for serving creamed food of any kind.

Bow Knots: Cut strips of bread $\frac{3}{4}$-inch wide, $10\frac{1}{2}$ inches long. Tie once gently, brush with melted·butter, then toast in hot oven. Serve on a salad plate.

Toasted Bread Baskets: Cut bread in $2\frac{1}{2}$-inch thick slices, trimming off all crusts and cutting out the middle portion, leaving a square opening at the top. Toast and fill opening with creamed mixture. If made before needed, reheat before using.

Quick Breads
and Muffins

Orange-Nut Bread

1 medium-sized orange	2 cups flour
1 cup raisins or dates	¼ tsp. salt
2 tbsps. melted shortening	1 tsp. baking powder
1 tsp. vanilla	½ tsp. soda
1 egg, well beaten	1 cup sugar
	½ cup chopped nuts

Pour juice from orange into an 8-oz. measuring cup; add boiling water to fill cup. Remove membrane from orange peel. Put peel and raisins through food chopper, using coarse blade. Add diluted orange juice. Stir in shortening, vanilla and egg. Add flour sifted with salt, baking powder, soda and sugar. Mix well and stir in nuts. Bake in greased loaf pan in moderate oven 350 degrees for 1 hour.

Lemon Bread

½ cup butter or shortening	1 tsp. baking powder
1 cup sugar	½ tsp. salt
2 eggs, unbeaten	½ cup chopped nuts
½ cup milk	Grated rind of 1 lemon
1½ cups flour	

Cream shortening, add sugar and cream well. Add eggs, 1 at a time, beating well after each addition. Add sifted dry ingredients alternately with milk and lastly the nuts and lemon rind. Bake in loaf pan in oven 350 degrees for about 1 hour. When done pour syrup slowly over loaf and return to oven and bake a few minutes longer. Raisins added to this loaf will improve the flavor and look.

Syrup: Make a syrup by bringing to a good boil the juice of 1 lemon and ¼ cup sugar.

Cherry Bread

Butter, size of an egg
1 cup brown sugar
1 egg, beaten
2 cups flour
2 tsps. baking powder

½ tsp. salt
½ cup chopped walnuts
1 small bottle cherries, sliced
Milk

Cream butter and sugar. Add egg and blend well. Put juice of bottle of cherries into cup and fill with milk to make 1 cup. Add this liquid alternately with sifted dry ingredients, and lastly the chopped nuts and cherries. Put into greased loaf pan and let rise for 20 minutes before putting into oven. Bake about ¾ hour at 375 degrees, lowering heat after the first 15 minutes.

Pineapple Bread

½ cup butter
½ cup sugar
2 eggs
2 cups flour
3 tsps. baking powder

¼ tsp. soda
½ cup candied cherries, cut
¾ cup drained crushed pineapple
⅓ cup pineapple juice

Cream well first three ingredients. Add the sifted dry ingredients alternately with the pineapple juice, and with the last addition of flour add the cherries and pineapple. Bake in greased loaf pan at 325 degrees for about 1 hour.

Banana Bread

½ cup butter
1 cup sugar
2 eggs, beaten
2½ cups flour

½ cup cold water
1 tsp. soda
1 tsp. baking powder
1 cup mashed banana pulp

Cream the butter, sugar, and eggs. Add the sifted dry ingredients in about three parts to the sugar mixture, alternating with the water and banana pulp. Bake in greased loaf pan at 350 degrees for about 1 hour.

Variation: Add 1 cup raisins or ½ cup nuts.

Coconut Bread

⅓ cup butter
1 cup sugar
2 eggs, beaten
1 cup milk
2¼ cups flour

2 (less) cups fine coconut
1 tsp. vanilla
⅛ tsp. salt
3 tsps. baking powder
Red and green cherries, cut small

Cream the first three ingredients. Sift the dry ingredients several times and add to creamed mixture alternately with milk. Lastly add the coconut and cherries. Bake in greased loaf pan at 350 degrees, just to a medium golden brown. Do not overbake.

All Bran Banana Bread

¼ cup shortening
¼ cup sugar
1 egg, well beaten
1 cup All Bran
1½ cups all purpose flour

1½ cups mashed banana
2 tsps. baking powder
½ tsp. salt
½ tsp. soda

Cream sugar and shortening. Add well beaten egg, All Bran and mashed banana. Lastly add the flour which has been well sifted with baking powder, salt, and soda. Bake in moderate oven for about one hour.

Cranberry Bread

⅓ cup shortening
2 eggs
1¼ cups sugar
2¼ cups flour
1½ tsps. baking powder

1 tsp. soda
1 tsp. salt
1 cup raw cranberries, sliced
¾ cup chopped walnuts
Grated rind and juice of 1 orange

Squeeze juice of orange and put into measuring cup. Fill cup with hot water. Add shortening and set aside to cool. Beat eggs until thick and beat in sugar gradually. Alternately add dry ingredients and orange juice mixture. Fold in combined cranberries, orange rind and nuts. Put into greased loaf pan and bake in oven 350 degrees for about 1 hour.

Note: The addition of yellow and green chopped pineapple makes this loaf very colorful and delicious.

Date Bread

Mix all together and boil until it begins to fizz.

1 cup dates   2 tbsps. butter
1 cup chopped walnuts   ¾ cup water
1 tsp. soda

   Add:

   1 cup brown sugar   1½ cups flour
   1 egg, beaten   1 tsp. vanilla
   ¼ cup milk

Turn into greased loaf pan and bake in oven 350 degrees for 35-40 minutes.

Raisin Bread

1 cup seedless raisins   1 cup sugar
Thin rind of 2 oranges   1 egg, beaten
Juice of 2 oranges   2 cups flour
1 tbsp. melted butter   1 tsp. baking powder
Boiling water   ½ tsp. soda
                               ½ tsp. salt

Put raisins and rind through food chopper, using a very fine blade. Add butter. Put juice into cup and add boiling water to make 1 level cup. Pour this over the mixture. Add egg, sugar, and well sifted dry ingredients.

Bake for 1 hour in oven 350 degrees.

Quick Bran Bread

2 cups all-bran   2 cups flour
2 cups sour milk   2 tsps. soda
2 tsps. molasses   1 tsp. salt
½ cup sugar

Mix the first four ingredients; add sifted dry ingredients. Mix quickly and pour into greased loaf pan. Bake in moderate oven 350 degrees.

Corn Bread (Johnny Cake)

1 cup flour	1 cup corn meal
2 tbsps. sugar	1 egg
4 tsps. baking powder	1 cup milk
½ tsp. salt	1 tbsp. melted butter

Sift well the dry ingredients. Add corn meal. Beat egg, add milk and add to the flour mixture. Mix thoroughly and add melted butter. Bake in an 8-inch square pan for 30 minutes. This bread is best when spread generously with butter.

Tea Ring

1¾ cups flour	4 tbsps. shortening
4 tsps. baking powder	1 egg, beaten
½ tsp. salt	3 tbsps. milk
¼ cup sugar	

Sift together dry ingredients. Put into mixing bowl and with pastry blender cut in shortening. Combine slightly beaten egg and milk; mix lightly but thoroughly. Knead dough, a few moments only, on floured board or canvas and roll out in ⅓-inch rectangle. Sprinkle with the following mixture:

¾ cup brown sugar
2 tsps. cinnamon
2 tbsps. melted butter

On top of this sprinkle some seedless raisins, nut meats and some cut up cherries or peel. Roll up as for jelly roll and pinch ends together to form ring. Using scissors, cut to within ½-inch of inside edge at 1½-inch intervals; separate slices, twisting to one side, as you do so. Brush top lightly with milk and sprinkle with a little granulated sugar. Bake in oven 400 degrees for about 25 minutes. When cold ice and sprinkle with chopped fruit and nuts.

French Coffee Cake

4 cups flour	1 yeast cake
¼ cup sugar	¼ cup warm water
1 tsp. salt	2 tsps. cinnamon
1 cup warm milk	1 cup sugar
3 eggs, separated	1 cup chopped nuts
½ lb. butter or margarine	1¼ cups confectioner's sugar

Sift together flour, sugar and salt. Cut in butter until the size of small peas. Add warm milk and well beaten egg yolks, stirring until soft dough is formed. Add yeast, dissolved in warm water. Beat and let stand in refrigerator over night. Divide dough in two parts. Roll each half in a rectangular shape on floured canvas to ¼-inch thickness. Spread each part with stiffly beaten egg whites. Sprinkle with a mixture of cinnamon, sugar and nuts. Roll as for jelly roll and place in greased pans. Keep in warm place until loaves are double in bulk. Bake in oven 350 degrees for about 45 minutes. Frost, while warm, with confectioner's sugar icing, blending sugar with enough milk or cream to a thin spreading consistency.

Note: Instead of icing the cake add some of the icing sugar to the egg whites. The addition of some cut citron and cherries makes this extra nice.

Cut this very special cake in king-size portions.

Quick Coffee Cake

¾ cup sugar
¾ cup butter or margarine
1 egg
½ cup milk

1½ cups flour
2 tsps. baking powder
½ tsp. salt

Sift dry ingredients into mixing bowl. Cut in shortening. Add beaten egg and milk; beat until smooth. Spread in 8-inch square pan and sprinkle top with a mixture of:

½ cup brown sugar, 1 tsp. cinnamon, 1 tbsp. melted butter, ½ cup nuts. Bake in oven 375 degrees for 30-35 minutes. Serve warm.

Muffins (Basic Recipe)

1½ cups flour
4 tsps. baking powder
1 tbsp. sugar
½ tsp. salt

2 eggs, well beaten
¾ cup milk
¼ cup melted shortening

Sift dry ingredients into mixing bowl and make a well in the center. Combine liquids; add, all at once, and stir just until dry ingredients are moistened but not smooth. Batter should be lumpy. Unnecessary beating results in tough muffins. Fill greased preheated muffin tins two-thirds full. Bake in hot oven 425 degrees for about 20 minutes.

Surprise Muffins: Fill muffin tins half full of batter. Drop a scant teaspoonful of jelly or jam on center of batter. Add more batter to fill tins two-thirds full.

Raspberry or Blueberry Muffins: Reduce milk to ½ cup and add 1 cup fresh raspberries or blueberries to sifted dry ingredients, being careful not to crush fruit.

Raisin, Date or Nut Muffins: Add ½ to ¾ cup seedless raisins, broken nuts or coarsely chopped dates to basic recipe.

Sour Milk Muffins: Substitute ¾ cup sour milk or buttermilk for sweet milk. Add ½ tsp. soda and reduce baking powder to 2 teaspoons. Soda and baking powder are sifted with dry ingredients. Bake as directed in basic recipe.

Oatmeal Buttermilk Muffins: 1 cup sifted flour, ¼ cup sugar, 2 tsps. baking powder, ½ tsp. soda, ½ tsp. salt, 1 well beaten egg, 3 tbsps. melted shortening, 1 cup quick cooking rolled oats, 1 cup buttermilk. Mix and bake by the same method as for basic recipe.

Cornmeal Muffins: Using basic recipe reduce flour to ¾ cup and add ¾ cup cornmeal.

Carrot Muffins: 2 cups flour, 4 tsps. baking powder, ½ tsp. salt, 2 tbsps. sugar, 1 cup grated raw carrot, 1 egg, 1 cup milk, 3 tbsps. melted shortening. Sift dry ingredients; add carrot. Beat egg, add milk and melted shortening. Make a well in dry ingredients. Pour in the egg mixture and mix quickly. Batter should be lumpy. Fill tins two-thirds full.

Sour Cream Muffins: 1½ cups flour, 1 tsp. baking powder, ¼ tsp. soda, ¼ tsp. salt, 2 tbsps. sugar, 1 egg, 1 cup sour cream, 1 tbsp. melted butter. Sift dry ingredients together; add beaten egg, cream, butter, and mix quickly. Fill muffin tins two-thirds full. Bake in oven 400 degrees for about 20 minutes.

Bran Muffins: Cut up 1 cup dates. Add ½ cup raisins and ½ cup boiling water. Cover and keep over medium heat for 10 minutes. Cream 1 rounded tbsp. shortening; add 1 cup molasses and 1 egg. Beat well. Add 1 cup bran flakes, 1 cup flour that has been sifted with 2 dessertspoons baking powder and ½ tsp. salt. Add date and raisin mixture and at the same time just enough milk to make a fairly thin batter. Bake as for basic mixture.

Pumpkin Muffins

1 egg
½ cup cooked mashed or
    canned pumpkin
½ cup milk
4 tbsps. melted butter
1½ cups flour
½ cup sugar

2 tsps. baking powder
½ tsp. salt
½ tsp. cinnamon
½ tsp. nutmeg
½ cup seedless raisins

Preheat oven to 400 degrees. Grease 12 muffin cups. Sift together several times the flour, baking powder, salt, spice, sugar. Beat egg slightly with a fork and stir in milk, pumpkin, and melted butter. Add dry ingredients. Batter will be lumpy. Fill muffin cups with batter and sprinkle each one with ¼ tsp. sugar. Bake 18 to 20 minutes.

Banana Muffins

2 large bananas, crushed
⅔ cup white sugar
1 egg, beaten
1½ cups flour

1 tsp. soda
1 tsp. baking powder
5½ tbsps. corn oil
½ tsp. salt

Crush bananas and add sugar. Mix well. Add beaten egg. Add dry ingredients. Add oil lastly and bake at 375 for about 20 minutes.

Tea Biscuits

2 cups flour
4 tsps. baking powder
½ tsp. salt

4 tbsps. butter
¾ cup milk

Sift dry ingredients; cut in butter until mixture resembles coarse crumbs.

Add milk, all at once, and mix quickly. Turn out on lightly floured canvas and knead gently about one-half minute. (A little kneading produces flaky biscuits with a finer texture but too much kneading makes biscuits tough). Pat to required thickness, and cut with biscuit cutter. Bake in hot oven 425 degrees for about 12 minutes.

Note: 2 tsps. cream of tartar and 1 tsp. soda may be used to replace baking powder.

Filled Tea Biscuits: Cut biscuits about ¼-inch thick. Brush half the rounds with melted butter. Spread the buttered rounds with any savory meat filling or sweet filling as jam, marmalade, or cheese. Press plain round on top, brush with milk and bake.

Orange Biscuits; Add grated peel of 1 orange to basic recipe. Dip cube of loaf sugar quickly in orange juice and press gently into the center of each biscuit. Bake as directed. If preferred, the juice of the orange may be added but keep the liquid to ¾ cup.

Cheese Biscuits: Roll biscuit dough to ¼-inch thickness. Sprinkle over it ½ cup grated cheese and some finely chopped pimiento. Roll up and cut in ½-inch slices. Bake, cut side down, in hot oven 425 degrees for 12 minutes.

Note: An easier method for making Cheese Biscuits is by adding about ⅓ cup grated cheese to dry ingredients.

Scones

3 cups flour   ½ cup shortening
2 tbsps. sugar   1 cup milk
4 tsps. baking powder   1 egg
½ tsp. salt

Sift dry ingredients into mixing bowl. Blend in shortening. Beat egg, add milk and add this to the flour mixture, combining ingredients with a few swift strokes. Handle dough as little as possible. Pat to ¾-inch thickness, on floured canvas. Cut in diamond shapes, brush with milk and bake in oven 450 degrees for about 15 minutes.

Popovers

2 eggs   ½ tsp. salt
1 cup mlk   1 tbsp. melted butter
⅞ cup flour

Beat eggs thoroughly. Add milk, then the sifted dry ingredients. Add butter and beat for one minute with rotary or electric beater. Pour into sizzling hot muffin tins or ovenproof custard cups (the latter preferred), and bake for about 45 minutes. Start in a hot oven 475 degrees for the first 15 minutes, decreasing heat to 350 degrees to finish baking. A few minutes before removing from oven, prick to let steam escape. Serve hot from oven, with butter.

Drop Date Doughnuts

3 eggs
1 cup sugar
1 cup milk
2½ cups flour

2 tsps. baking powder
1 tsp. salt
1 tsp. vanilla

Beat eggs very stiff and beat in sugar gradually. Add milk and vanilla and lastly the flour sifted with baking powder and salt. Lay pitted dates on top of batter and with a spoon cover each one with the batter. Drop quickly in sizzling hot fat and fry. Roll in sugar while warm.

Orange Doughnuts

4 eggs
¾ cup milk
¼ cup orange juice
Rind of 1 orange

1¼ cups sugar
4½ cups flour
4 tsps. baking powder
½ tsp. salt
5 tbsps. melted shortening

Beat eggs well. Add milk and orange juice; blend well. Add the melted shortening and sifted dry ingredients. Chill for 1 hour. Roll out on canvas and cut. Fry in hot fat 370 degrees. Drain and roll in sugar.

Old Fashioned Doughnuts

3 eggs
1½ cups sugar
8 tbsps. melted shortening
5 cups all-purpose flour

1 tsp. salt
3 tbsps. baking powder
1 tbsp. vanilla
1½ cups milk

Beat eggs well and add sugar gradually while beating. Add vanilla and melted shortening. Sift dry ingredients and add alternately with milk, ending with flour. Roll out on lightly flour canvas or board and cut with cutter in desired shape. Fry in pan of shortening, heated until it barely begins to smoke. Drop in doughnuts and turn over immediately when they come to surface. When brown, turn again. Drain on cookie sheet covered with paper towel.

Raised Doughnuts

Make a sponge with these ingredients. Let rise for 1½ hours.

2½ cups milk, scalded and   2 tbsps. sugar
    cooled   1 yeast cake
1 cup flour

Mix ½ cup melted shortening, 1¼ cups sugar, 2 eggs (beaten), 1 tsp. salt. 1 tsp. each of lemon extract and nutmeg and add to above mixture. Add enough flour to make a soft dough. Let rise about 2 hours. Roll out to a thickness of ½ inch. Cut out with round or diamond shape cutter. Let rise until light, and fry in deep fat.

Jelly Doughnuts: Cut the dough in 2½-inch rounds. Place on one round a teaspoonful of jelly or jam, cap with another round, brush edges with milk or egg white and seal. Fry as directed.

Cakes, Cookies and Squares

When company drops in, nothing compares
With a treat of good cake, cookies or squares.

White Fruit Cake

1½ cups butter
1½ cups white sugar
6 eggs, well beaten
½ cup orange juice
Grated rind of 1 orange
1½ tsps. vanilla
3½ cups all purpose flour
1 tsp. baking powder

1 tsp. salt
¼ lb. almonds, blanched and
    slivered
1 cup white raisins
¼ lb. candied pineapple
¾ lb. candied cherries (red and
    green) cut in halves
¼ lb. citron

Soak cut up fruit overnight in orange juice, rind and vanilla. Cream butter; add sugar gradually and beat well. Add well beaten eggs; beat until light and fluffy. Add the sifted flour, baking powder and salt to mixture and mix until well blended. Add fruit. If cake is not to be iced place whole blanched almonds on top before baking. Bake in square pan at 225-250 degree oven. When baking fruit cake place pan of water in oven. This cake is a delight to serve and is much improved after the first week.

Sugar Plum Fruit Cake

1½ cups dried apricots
¼ cup honey
1 cup seeded raisins
¼ cup brandy or grapejuice
1 cup diced candied pineapple
1 cup candied cherries, halved
1½ cups diced citron
1 cup diced candied orange
    peel
1 cup sliced dates
1 cup slivered blanched
    almonds

2 cups seedless raisins
1 cup coarsely chopped walnuts
1 cup coarsely chopped pecans
1 cup butter or shortening
1¼ cups brown sugar
4 eggs
2 cups flour
1 tsp. salt
½ tsp. mace
¼ tsp. cloves
¼ tsp. soda
1 tsp. cinnamon

Rinse apricots; cover with water and boil 10 minutes. Drain, cool and chop. Combine with honey in small pan and bring to boiling point. Cover and let stand until cool. Rinse both seeded and seedless raisins and drain well. Chop seeded raisins. Turn apricots and honey into large bowl; add raisins and pour brandy over all ingredients. Cover and let stand overnight. Candied fruit, citron, dates and nuts may be prepared and added to this bowl the same day but do not mix so that dried fruits soak in brandy and honey. The next day cream shortening and sugar thoroughly. Beat in eggs, 1 at a time. Sift flour, salt, soda and spices and mix thoroughly into creamed mixture. Now mix fruits in large bowl by lifting from bottom of bowl with large spoon. Pour batter over fruits and mix very well. Turn into greased pans lined with greased brown or wax paper. Use one 10-inch tube cake pan or a large loaf pan. Bake in slow oven 275 degrees for 4-5 hours. Makes 6½ to 7 lbs. cake. After cake has cooled completely, wrap in cloth dipped in brandy, and then wrap in aluminum foil. Store cake in tin to age for four or more weeks.

Pound Cake

1 lb. butter
1 lb. sugar
1 lb. eggs (8 large)
1 lb. (scant) flour (3¾ cups)
½ tsp. baking powder

1 tsp. salt
½ tsp. grated lemon rind
2 tbsps. lemon juice
½ tsp. lemon extract
½ tsp. mace

Cream butter; add sugar slowly and cream well. Add flavoring and well beaten egg yolks. Sift together flour, baking powder, salt, mace and add to mixture. Beat, only until smooth, then fold in the beaten egg whites. Bake in a loaf pan lined with several layers of brown paper. Grease the top layer with butter. Tie a piece of brown paper over top of pan and bake in a slow oven 300 degrees for 2 hours. Remove paper and bake a little longer, if necessary.

Cold Water Pound Cake

1 cup butter	3 cups flour
2 cups sugar	1 tsp. cream of tartar
1 cup cold water	½ tsp. soda
3 eggs, unbeaten	Flavoring to taste

Cream butter and sugar well. Add eggs, 1 at a time, beating well after each addition, as upon this depends the quality of the cake. Sift dry ingredients several times and add alternately with water. Add flavoring. Bake in oven 325 degrees. This makes a large loaf.

Pineapple Cake (For a crowd)

1 can (14 oz. size) crushed pineapple	½ cup shortening
1 cup flaked coconut	Dash ginger
2 cups flour	¾ cup sugar
1 tsp. baking powder	2 eggs
½ tsp. soda	1 6-oz pkg. semi-sweet
¼ tsp. salt	chocolate pieces

Preheat oven to 375 degrees. Grease a 15 × 10 inch pan. Mix ¾ cup of undrained pineapple with coconut and set aside. Sift flour, soda, baking powder, salt and ginger together. Work shortening until soft; gradually work in sugar until mixture is creamy. Add eggs, 1 at a time, and beat hard after each addition. Add flour mixture and remaining undrained pineapple alternately to the batter. Lastly, mix in chocolate pieces. Pour into baking pan, sprinkle batter with pineapple-coconut topping and bake 25 minutes or until cake pulls away from the sides of the pan. When cool, cut in 3 × 2 inch pieces. This makes about 25 servings.

Rhubarb Cake

2 eggs, beaten
1½ cups white sugar
½ cup margarine
½ cup milk

1½ tsps. baking powder
1½ cup white flour
2 cups rhubarb, cut fine and
     floured
Dash of salt and vanilla

Bake in the usual way and top with ¼ cup white sugar and 1 tsp. cinnamon mixed together. Sprinkle on cake while warm.

Golden Chiffon Cake

Measure and sift together in mixing bowl:

1 cup cake flour, sifted several
     times
¾ cup sugar

1½ tsps. baking powder
½ tsp. salt

Make a well and add:

¼ cup mazola
3 egg yolks

⅜ cup (¼ cup plus 2 tbsps.) cold
     water or orange juice
1 tsp. vanilla or 1 tsp. grated
     orange rind

Beat above with spoon until smooth. In another bowl measure ½ cup egg whites (3 or 4), ¼ tsp. cream of tartar. Whip until very stiff. Pour egg yolk mixture gradually over egg whites, gently folding until just blended. Pour into an ungreased angel cake or 8 or 9-inch square pan and bake at 300 degrees for 30-40 minutes. Invert pan as soon as taken from oven so that cake does not touch and let stand until cold. The success of this cake depends on the slow baking.

Birthday Cake

¾ cup butter
¼ cut shortening
2 cups sugar
3 eggs, unbeaten
3 cups flour

2 tsps. baking powder
1 tsp. each lemon and vanilla
1 tsp. salt
½ cup milk
½ cup hot water

Cream butter and shortening well. Add sugar gradually and cream well. Then gradually beat in milk, hot water and flavoring. After each cup of flour, add 1 egg and to the third cup of flour add the baking powder. Fruit or nuts may be added. Bake for 1 hour at 375 degrees, lowering temperature to 300 degrees after the first half hour. (I use the electric mixer for satisfactory results).

Orange Rum Cake

Assemble ingredients and let stand 1 hour.

1 cup butter or margarine
(salted, not whipped)
2 cups granulated sugar
Grated rind of 2 large oranges
and 1 lemon
2 eggs
2½ cups sifted all purpose
flour
2 tsps. double action baking
powder
1 tsp. baking soda

½ tsp. salt
1 cup buttermilk
1 cup finely chopped walnuts or
pecans
Juice of 2 large oranges
Juice of 1 lemon
2 tbsps. rum
½ cup confectioners sugar
Walnut or pecan halves

With a little butter grease a 9 × 10 inch tube pan. Set oven 350 degrees. With an electric mixer or large spoon beat 1 cup butter in a large bowl until fluffy. Gradually add 1 cup granulated sugar and beat after each addition until fluffy. Add grated rind of 2 large oranges and 1 lemon. Add 2 eggs, one at a time, and beat after each addition until very light. Put 2½ cups sifted flour into sifter. Add 2 tsps. double acting baking powder, 1 tsp. baking soda, ½ tsp. salt. Sift into bowl. To butter mixture add flour mixture alternately with 1 cup buttermilk in small amounts, beating after each addition until smooth. Fold in 1 cup finely chopped walnuts or pecans. Pour batter into pan. Bake about one hour. Cake is done when it shrinks from sides of pan and springs back when pressed lightly with finger. Meanwhile, strain juice of 2 large oranges and 1 lemon into saucepan. Add 1 cup granulated sugar and 2 tbsps. rum. When cake is done, remove from oven. Bring mixture in saucepan to boil; pour slowly over cake in pan. If cake does not absorb all of mixture as it is poured, reserve remainder. Spoon on later. Let cake stand a day or two before serving. Remove cake from pan. Sprinkle cake lightly with granulated sugar, if desired. Mix ¾ cup confectioner's sugar with a little water or milk to make of spreading consistency. Spread on nut halves; let stand until hard. You will receive many raves for this cake!

To Store the Cake: Cover loosely with foil. Stored this way cake will keep for weeks.

All-At-Once Cake

¾ cup sugar
⅓ cup butter
1 cup flour

1 tsp. vanilla
2 eggs
1 tsp. baking powder
Milk

Put softened butter in measuring cup. Add two unbeaten eggs and fill cup with milk. Put all ingredients into a mixing bowl and beat altogether for 5 minutes. Bake in moderate oven 350 degrees.

Coconut Top Cake

½ cup butter or shortening
1½ cups sugar
3 egg yolks, beaten
1 tsp. cornstarch

1 cup flour
1 tsp. baking powder
¼ tsp. salt
5 tbsps. milk

Cream shortening and sugar; add egg yolks and blend well. Sift together the cornstarch, flour, baking powder and salt, and add alternately with milk. Spread the batter lightly with orange marmalade and cover with meringue made of the beaten egg whites, ½ cup sugar, 1 tsp. cornstarch, 1½ cups coconut. Bake in 8-inch square pan at 350 degrees for 45 minutes.

Prune Cake

1 cup vegetable oil
1½ cups sugar
3 eggs
2 cups flour
1 tsp. soda

½ tsp. nutmeg
1 cup buttermilk
1 tsp. vanilla
1 cup prunes, (cooked, seeded
    and chopped)
½ cup chopped nuts

Sift dry ingredients together. Blend well the sugar and oil. Add eggs, 1 at a time, beating well. Add dry ingredients, alternating with buttermilk. Add vanilla and stir in nuts and prunes which have been floured (a small amount of flour). Bake in a greased 8 × 12 or larger pan for 45 minutes at 300 degrees. Leave in pan.

Icing for Prune Cake:

1 cup sugar
1 tbsp. corn syrup
¼ cup butter
½ cup buttermilk

1 tsp. vanilla
½ tsp. nutmeg
½ tsp. soda

Combine all ingredients in large saucepan. Start cooking soon after cake is put into oven. Cook to soft ball stage, watching carefully. Cool slightly and pour over cake as soon as it comes from the oven.

Zucchini Cake

3 cups sifted flour	4 eggs
2 tsps. baking powder	2 cups sugar
1 tsp. soda	1½ cups corn oil
½ tsp. salt	3 cups grated zucchini
2 tsps. cinnamon	1 cups nuts or raisins

Mix well the first five ingredients. Beat eggs well and add sugar gradually. Add corn oil and mix well. Add to flour mixture. Lastly add the zucchini which should be drained, if watery. You may add half nuts and raisins, if desired. This makes a large loaf and keeps well.

Applesauce Cake

½ cup shortening	½ tsp. soda
1½ cups sugar	1 tsp. baking powder
2 eggs, beaten	¼ tsp. salt
1 cup thick unsweetened	1 tsp. cinnamon
applesauce	½ tsp. ground cloves
2 cups flour	1 cup seeded raisins, chopped

Cream shortening and sugar. Add eggs and beat well. Add applesauce and then the sifted dry ingredients. Fold in raisins. Beat smooth and bake in 8-inch square cake pan in oven 350 degrees, for 50-55 minutes.

War Cake

1 pkg. seeded raisins	2 cups brown sugar
2 tbsps. lard	1 tbsp. salt
2 cups hot water	

Boil above ingredients for 3 minutes. When cold add 1½ cups flour which has been sifted with 1 tsp. baking powder, 1 tsp. soda, 1 tsp. cinnamon, 1 tsp. cloves.

Bake for about 1 hour in moderate oven or longer, if necessary.

Blueberry Cake

2 eggs	1 tbsp. baking powder
¾ cup sugar	1 tbsp. melted butter
3 cups flour	1½ cups milk
¾ tsp. salt	1 cup blueberries

Beat eggs well and add sugar gradually. Add melted butter. Add the sifted dry ingredients alternately with milk. Lastly add the blueberries. Beat quickly and pour into a large buttered cake pan. Bake in a hot oven 400 degrees. Makes about 21 squares.

The Perfect Chocolate Cake

½ cup shortening	¼ tsp. baking powder
1 cup white sugar	2 squares melted chocolate
1 egg	1 tsp. vanilla
1 cup sour milk	1¾ cups pastry flour
1 tsp. baking soda (dissolved in sour milk)	½ tsp. salt

Cream shortening, add sugar gradually and beat until creamy and light. Add egg and beat well. Add melted chocolate and vanilla. Then add remaining dry ingredients alternately with milk. Pour into 8 × 8 cake pan which has been lined with greased wax paper. Bake in 350 degree oven.

Watermelon Cake

1 cup butter	2½ cups flour
1½ cups granulated sugar	1½ tsps. baking powder
3 eggs	Strawberry flavoring
¾ cup cold water	

Cream butter and sugar well. Add eggs, one at a time, beating well after each addition. Sift flour with baking powder and add alternately with water, stirring just until the water and flour has disappeared in batter. Take out ⅓ batter, color with red coloring, add ½ cup raisins and strawberry flavoring. Put raisin batter in bottom of well greased and floured angel cake pan and the plain batter on top. Bake in 350° oven about 1 hour. Ice with butter icing, tinted with green coloring.

Quick Marble Cake

½ cup butter or shortening
1¼ cups sugar
1¾ cups cake flour
3 tsps. baking powder
1 tsp. salt
¾ cup milk

2 eggs, unbeaten
1 tsp. vanilla
1 square unsweetened chocolate,
    melted
¼ tsp. soda
3 tbsps. boiling water

Put the first six ingredients into a bowl and beat by hand for 2 minutes. Add eggs and vanilla and beat 1 minute longer. Divide in two parts. To one part, add the melted chocolate which has been mixed with soda and water. Grease a 9-inch tube pan. Place large spoonfuls of batter in it, alternating the light and the dark. Bake for about 1 hour in a moderate oven 350 degrees.

Date-Nut Cake

1 cup dates, sliced
1 tsp. soda
1 cup boiling water
½ cup butter
¼ tsp. salt

1 cup sugar
1 egg, beaten
2 cups flour (scant)
1 tsp. vanilla
½ cup chopped walnuts

Cut up dates; add soda and boiling water and let stand to cool. In another bowl cream butter and sugar; add egg and beat well. Add flour and salt alternately with the water from dates. Add vanilla, dates and nuts. Bake in tube pan about 55 minutes in oven 350 degrees. This is a rather thin batter.

Icing: Cream 1 small pkg. cream cheese and blend in icing sugar. Add a little cream or milk, if necessary.

Lemon Layer Cake

½ cup butter or shortening
1 cup sugar
3 egg yolks, well beaten
2 cups cake flour

1 tsp. grated lemon rind
3 tsps. baking powder
¼ tsp. salt
¾ cup milk

Cream butter, add sugar and blend until quite creamy. Add and stir in well the beaten egg yolks and lemon rind. Add the sifted dry ingredients alternately with milk, beginning and ending with flour; beat well after each addition. Bake in greased 9-inch layer pans in oven 375 degrees. Put together with Lemon Filling. Ice with lemon icing, or dust with powdered sugar.

Hot Milk Cake

3 eggs
1 cup sugar
1 cup cake flour
6 tbsps. milk, heated

1 tsp. baking powder
⅛ tsp. salt
1 tsp. vanilla or almond extract

Beat eggs until thick and lemon colored; add sugar gradually, beating constantly. Add flavoring and the sifted dry ingredients and lastly, beat in the hot milk. Bake in oven 350 degrees. This cake is nice topped with a boiled icing and sprinkled with crushed peanuts.

Surprise Sponge Cake

2 eggs, separated
1¼ cups sugar
1½ cups cake flour
1 tsp. vanilla

⅔ cup cold water
½ tsp. baking powder
¼ tsp. salt

Put egg yolks and water into large bowl and beat until it foams up about the size of a quart. Add the sifted sugar and beat for 7 minutes. Add flour, baking powder and salt, sifted together several times; beat well. Fold in the beaten egg whites. Bake in pan 8 × 10 in moderate oven.

Sponge Cake

1 cup cake flour
¼ tsp. salt
Grated rind of ½ lemon
1½ tbsps. lemon juice

5 egg yolks
5 egg whites
1 cup sugar

Sift flour and salt together several times. Add lemon rind and juice to beaten yolks and beat until thick and lemon colored. Beat whites until stiff but not dry. Fold in sugar, a small amount at a time, then add egg yolk mixture. Fold in flour gently with a rubber spatula until all is used. Pour batter into a 9-inch ungreased tube pan and bake for 1 hour in oven 350 degrees. Remove from oven and invert pan for 1 hour before removing cake.

Devil's Food Cake

¾ cup shortening
1⅞ cups brown sugar
3 eggs, beaten
¾ cup boiling water
3 oz. unsweetened chocolate
2¼ cups cake flour

1½ tsps. soda
¾ tsp. baking powder
¾ tsp. salt
¾ cup sour milk
1 tsp. vanilla

Cream shortening well; add sugar and cream until quite fluffy. Add the well beaten eggs and blend well. Pour boiling water over chocolate and melt over heat until smooth. Cool and add to egg mixture; blend thoroughly. Sift flour with dry ingredients; add to chocolate mixture alternately with milk and flavoring. Pour batter into greased loaf or layer pans. Bake layers 30-35 minutes and in loaf pan 40-45 minutes in oven 350 degrees.

Angel Cake

1¼ cups sugar
1 cup cake flour
1 cup egg whites (8 to 10 eggs)
1 tsp. cream of tartar

½ tsp. salt
¾ tsp. vanilla
¼ tsp. almond extract

Sift the ¼ cup of sugar and the flour together 3 or 4 times. Beat egg whites, cream of tartar and salt to a stiff foam. Add remaining sugar gradually (rotary beater is best). Add flavorings. Fold in flour, sifting a little at a time over egg white and sugar mixture. Pour into a 9-inch ungreased tube pan and cut through batter, with a knife, to break up any air bubbles. Bake in oven 350 degrees for about 10 minutes, then reduce heat to 250 degrees to complete baking. Invert pan for 1 hour and remove cake.

Toughies (Childrens Delight)

Beat 2 eggs. Add 1 cup brown sugar and 1 cup molasses. Beat well. Add 2 tsps. soda dissolved in ¼ cup hot water, 1 tbsp. vinegar, 3 to 3½ cups flour, 1 tsp. each of cinnamon and ginger, ½ tsp. cloves, 1 tsp. salt. Add 2 tbsps. melted shortening to mixture. Drop on greased cookie sheet, well apart, and bake in oven 400 degrees.

Prize Jelly Roll

3 eggs, separated
1 cup sugar (scant)
2 tbsps. water
2 tbsps. orange juice
1 cup cake flour

1 tsp. baking powder
¼ tsp. salt
Grated rind of ½ orange
Jelly or jam

Beat the egg whites until stiff; add the beaten yolks and sugar. Blend thoroughly. Add the water, orange juice and grated rind. Fold in the well sifted dry ingredients. Line a cookie sheet or 8 × 12 inch pan with wax paper. Spread the batter evenly and bake in oven 350 degrees for about 15 minutes. While it is hot invert the pan onto a sheet of unglazed brown paper or a tea towel sprinkled with granulated or confectioner's sugar. Spread the cake sparingly with jelly or jam, and roll. Wrap roll in wax paper. Lemon filling may be used instead of jelly.

Spanish Bun

¾ cup shortening
3 eggs, separated
1½ cups brown sugar
1 cup milk
1 tsp. ginger

2 cups flour
3 tsps. baking powder
¼ tsp. salt
1 tsp. nutmeg
2 tsps. cinnamon

Cream shortening and sugar well. Add 1 whole egg and 2 egg yolks, well beaten, reserving the 2 egg whites for meringue topping. Add the flour sifted with salt and spices, alternately with milk, beginning and ending with flour. Bake in a shallow pan in oven 375 degrees for about 30 minutes.

Topping: Beat the two egg whites until stiff but not dry. Add ½ cup of brown sugar and blend well. Spread on top of cake, return to oven until meringue is lightly browned.

No-Bake Crunchies

¾ cup corn syrup
¾ cup white sugar

Let above come just to boiling point. Add 1 cup peanut butter (crunchy or plain) and mix well. Add 2 cups rice crispies and 2 cups cornflakes. Put in greased 8 × 8 inch pan and keep in refrigerator 2 hours before cutting.

Tiny Tim Fruitcake Cookies

½ cup shortening
1 cup brown sugar (packed)
1 tsp. salt
1 tsp. cinnamon
½ tsp. ground cloves
⅛ tsp. nutmeg
¼ tsp. soda

2 eggs
1 cup flour
¼ cup buttermilk or sour milk
1 cup currants
1 cup raisins
¾ cup dried mixed fruits
1 cup chopped nut meats

Cream shortening, sugar, salt and spices. Add eggs and beat until light. Mix in the sifted flour and soda, then buttermilk. Add remaining ingredients. Drop on greased cookie sheet and bake in moderate oven.

Cherry Surprises

½ cup butter
1 tsp. milk
1 tsp. vanilla

1½ cups icing sugar
1½ cups dessicated coconut

Mix above ingredients well. Wrap a little around a whole maraschino cherry and roll in finely crushed graham wafer crumbs. Keep in refrigerator. Nicer if cherries are marinated in rum for several hours.

Lemon Refrigerator Cookies

2 cups flour
¼ tsp. soda
½ tsp. salt
1 cup shortening
½ cup brown sugar

½ cup granulated sugar
1 egg, well beaten
2 tbsps. lemon juice
Grated rind of 1 lemon
½ cup chopped nut meats

Cream shortening until fluffy. Add brown and white sugar and cream well. Add egg, lemon juice and rind, and mix well. Add the sifted dry ingredients and nuts. Mix, and form into rolls. Wrap in wax paper and chill overnight. Cut with a sharp knife and bake in oven 375 degrees until a golden brown.

Choice Cheese Bits

1 cup pastry flour
¼ lb. butter

½ of an 8 oz. pkg. yellow cheese,
    grated

Mix well above ingredients. Roll out to desired thickness and cut in rounds. On one half of round put 1 tsp. pineapple marmalade. Fold over to form crescent. Seal edges with fork. Bake in moderate oven until lightly browned.

Ice-Box Cookies

1 cup butter
2 cups brown sugar
2 eggs
1 tsp. vanilla

3 cups flour
1 cup chopped raisins or nuts
1 tsp. soda
Chopped cherries or pineapple
    (optional)

Combine ingredients in the usual way and shape the dough into long rolls, about 2 inches in diameter. If the dough is too soft to roll, chill it until it may be handled easily. Cover the rolls with wax paper and chill for about 24 hours. Slice and bake on a greased baking sheet in oven 400 degrees for about 10 minutes.

Cream Cheese Ice-Box Cookies

½ cup butter or shortening
1 cup sugar
1 egg, well beaten
½ tsp. baking powder
2 cups flour

1 3-oz. pkg. cream cheese
2 tbsps. sour milk
1 tsp. lemon extract
⅛ tsp. soda
½ tsp. salt

Cream butter, sugar and egg. Add slightly softened cheese and beat it into the batter with the milk and lemon extract. Add the sifted dry ingredients and blend well. Form into rolls and wrap in wax paper. Chill. Slice, sprinkle with granulated sugar and bake in oven 400 degrees.

Note: Cinnamon added to the sugar makes a nice variation for topping.

Ice-Box Ginger Snaps

1 cup melted shortening	2½ cups flour (more, if necessary)
½ cup brown sugar	1 tsp. salt
2 tsps. soda	1½ tsps. ginger
¾ cup molasses	

Mix molasses and soda in bowl, stirring well. Add sugar and melted shortening, then the dry ingredients. Form into rolls and keep in refrigerator for several hours. Slice, and bake in oven about 400 degrees.

Prize Ginger Snaps

Boil 1 cup molasses and 2 tbsps. sugar for about 2 minutes. Add 1 tsp. ginger, ½ tsp. ground cloves, 1 tsp. soda, 4 tbsps. butter. When cooled a little, stir in 2½ cups (scant) flour, adding a bit more, if necessary. Roll very thin and bake quickly at 450 degrees.

Sugar Cookies

1 cup sugar	1 tsp. soda
1 cup butter	2 tsps. cream of tartar
2 eggs, well beaten	½ tsp. salt
2½ cups flour	Flavoring to taste

Combine ingredients in the usual way. Roll, not too thin and sprinkle with granulated sugar. Bake about 10 minutes in oven 375 degrees.

Variation: Press a raisin, nut meat, cherry or peel on top, or sprinkle with caraway seeds and press lightly with rolling pin.

Chocolate Chip Cookies

⅓ cup shortening	1 cup chocolate chips
⅓ cup margarine	1½ cups flour
½ cup brown sugar	½ tsp. soda
1 egg	½ tsp. salt

Cream shortening, margarine and sugar well. Sift flour, soda and salt several times. Beat egg well and add to shortening. Add sifted ingredients and chips. Drop about two inches apart on greased cookie sheet and bake in 375° oven about 10 mins. Raisins may also be added.

Magic Cookies

1 cup butter	2 cups flour
¾ cup brown sugar	⅞ tsp. salt
1 egg yolk	1 tsp. vanilla

Put small amount of batter on baking sheet. Press down with thumb and top with red or green cherries. Bake in moderate oven.

Rocky Mountain Peaks

2 eggs	1 tsp. butter
2 cups confectioner's sugar	1 cup chopped nut meats
4 squares unsweetened chocolate	20 marshmallows

Beat the eggs well; add sugar. Melt chocolate with butter and while hot add to egg and sugar mixture. Add nut meats and marshmallows, cut in pieces. Drop on wax paper and allow to stand for a few hours, until firm. Keep in cool place.

Almond Crisps

1 cup brown sugar	½ cup almonds, halved
½ cup butter, melted	1 tsp. almond extract
1 cup rolled oats	¼ tsp. salt
1 cup coconut	

Mix sugar and melted butter. Add other ingredients and mix well. Put into buttered pan 15 × 10 and bake in oven 350 degrees for about 20 minutes. Cut while warm; remove from pan when cold. This is quite soft when taken from oven but hardens as it cools.

Dandy Drop Cookies

1½ cups sugar	4 tbsps. sour milk
½ cup butter or shortening	1 tsp. soda
2 eggs, unbeaten	1 tsp. salt
1 tsp. cloves	2½ cups flour
1 tsp. cinnamon	

Cream sugar and shortening; add eggs and blend well. Sift together several times the dry ingredients and add alternately with milk, beginning and ending with flour. Bake in hot oven until a delicate brown.

Quick Ginger Snaps

1 cup sugar
¾ cup shortening
1 egg, unbeaten
4 tbsps. molasses
2 cups flour

2 tsps. soda
1 tsp. cinnamon
1 tsp. cloves
2 tsps. ginger

Cream sugar and shortening; add egg and molasses and blend well. Add the sifted dry ingredients. Form into balls and place on greased cookie sheet. Press with a fork and bake in a moderately hot oven.

Gumdrop Cookies

1 cup shortening
1 cup white sugar
1 cup brown sugar
2 eggs
2 cups flour
1 tsp. vanilla

1 tsp. baking powder
1 tsp. soda
½ tsp. salt
2 cups rolled oats
1 cup gumdrops (if large ones are
    used, cut)
½ cup coconut

Cream shortening, white and brown sugar; add beaten eggs. Stir in dry ingredients which have been sifted several times. Add vanilla, rolled oats, coconut and gumdrops. Pinch off small pieces of dough. Roll into 1-inch balls and flatten with a spatula dipped in milk. Bake cookies in a moderate oven 350 degrees, for about 10 minutes.

Mocha Coconut Patties

Combine and cook over moderate heat, stirring constantly until it has boiled 1 minute.

1½ cups light brown sugar
    (firmly packed)
1½ cups coconut
¼ tsp. salt

2 tbsps. butter
2 tbsps. instant coffee
⅓ cup water

Remove from heat.
Stir in 1 6-oz. package semi-sweet chocolate chips and let melt. Add ¼ tsp. almond flavoring. Drop by teaspoonfuls on wax paper or cookie sheet and chill until firm.

Note: Butterscotch chips and other flavorings make interesting variants.

Fruit Balls

½ cup cherries
1 lb. dates, cut
1 cup nut meats
1 cup coconut

1 egg, beaten
½ cup white sugar
4 tbsps. flour
¼ tsp. salt

Mix all together. Form into balls and bake in moderate oven, watching carefully. If balls separate while baking, pinch together. Roll in granulated sugar when cold. This is one of my prize Christmas cookies.

Special Oat Cakes

1½ cups sugar
2 cups rolled oats
2 cups flour
1 tsp. baking powder
1 tsp. salt

1¼ cups shortening
½ tsp. baking soda
½ cup boiling water
2 cups bran flakes

Add soda to boiling water and let stand until cool. Mix together flour, baking powder, salt, bran flakes, rolled oats and sugar. Cut in shortening. Add water and soda. Roll out thin on a floured board. Cut in rectangular shapes. Bake in a 350 degree oven until gold brown.

Scotch Cakes

1 cup butter
½ cup brown sugar

2 cups flour
1 tsp. vanilla

Cream well the butter and sugar. Add flavoring and flour; mix well. Roll out on lightly floured canvas and cut in desired shapes. Bake in slow oven 275 degrees until lightly browned.

Unbaked Cornflake Morsels

Boil together for 2 minutes:

Add:

¾ cup brown sugar
3½ tbsps. corn syrup
1 tbsp. butter

½ cup cut dates
½ cup coconut
2½ cups cornflakes

Mix above with the boiled mixture, shape like pyramids and place on wax paper. Put dab of peanut butter on top of each one and on top of this half a cherry.

Crunchy Crisps

1 cup shortening	1 cup coconut
1½ cups brown sugar	2 cups (scant) rolled oats
2 eggs, beaten	¼ tsp. soda
1½ cups flour	2 tsps. baking powder
2 cups cornflakes	¼ tsp. salt

Cream shortening and sugar well. Add eggs and the well sifted dry ingredients, cornflakes, coconut and rolled oats. Drop by teaspoonfuls on greased baking sheet and flatten with fork. Bake in moderate oven.

Molasses Spice Drops

½ cup white sugar	2 tsps. ginger
¾ cup shortening	1 tsp. cinnamon
1 egg	1 tsp. nutmeg
3 tbsps. molasses	2 tsps. soda
	Flour

Cream shortening and sugar. Add slightly beaten egg and blend well. Add molasses and spices and enough flour to make into soft balls. Roll balls in granulated sugar. Pat lightly with fork and bake in moderate oven 350 degrees for about 15 minutes.

A Favorite Molasses Cookie

1 cup molasses	1 tsp. ginger
1 cup granulated sugar	1 tsp. cloves
2 eggs, well beaten	1 tsp. salt
2 tsps. soda	

Dissolve soda in molasses. Add other ingredients, mix and chill for half an hour or longer. Mix in flour enough to make a soft dough, just manageable to roll out. Cut fairly thick and bake in moderate oven. This recipe requires no shortening.

Oat Cakes

2 cups rolled oats
1 cup flour
1 cup (scant) brown sugar

1 tsp. soda
½ tsp. salt
½ cup butter or drippings
Water enough to roll out

Combine dry ingredients; work shortening in with fingers. Add just enough water to hold together so that dough may be rolled. When rolling, instead of flour, use rolled oats on board. Cut in any desired shapes and bake in oven 350 degrees until lightly browned. Serve with or without butter.

Oatmeal Delights

½ cup butter or shortening
1 egg
1 cup flour
½ tsp. baking powder
1 cup raisins or finely cut
    dates
1 cup rolled oats

½ cup sugar
⅓ cup sour milk or buttermilk
¼ tsp. soda
½ tsp. salt
½ tsp. each of cinnamon and
    nutmeg
1 tsp. lemon juice

Cream shortening; add sugar and egg and mix well. Add other ingredients; blend well. Drop by teaspoonfuls on greased baking sheet. Make a dent in center of each and fill with jelly, jam, or a whole cherry. Bake in moderate oven.

Oatmeal Drop Cookies

½ cup butter or shortening
½ cup white sugar
½ cup brown sugar
1 egg, beaten
½ cup flour
1 tsp. vanilla

1 cup coconut
1 cup rolled oats
½ tsp. baking powder
½ tsp. soda
½ tsp. salt

Cream shortening with white and brown sugar. Add egg and mix well. Add the well sifted dry ingredients, coconut and rolled oats, vanilla. Drop from spoon on greased cookie sheet and flatten with fork. Bake in moderate oven until lightly browned.

Raisin Cup Cakes

1½ cups (or less) seedless Australian raisins. Cover with cold water and simmer for 20 minutes. Let cool. Keep water for addition to mixture later.

¾ cup brown sugar
¼ cup butter
1 egg
½ cup raisin water

1½ cups flour
1 tsp. soda
½ tsp. ground cloves
1 tsp. nutmeg
1 tsp. cinnamon

Cream butter and sugar. Add egg and raisin water. Add sifted dry ingredients and raisins. Bake in small size cup cake tins in oven 350 degrees. Do not over bake.

Perfect Raisin Drops

2 cups raisins
1 cup water
1 tsp. soda
1 cup shortening
2 cups sugar

3 eggs, beaten
4 cups flour
2 tsps. baking powder
1 tsp. cinnamon
1 tsp. salt
¼ tsp. nutmeg

Boil raisins and water for 5 minutes. Add soda to hot mixture and let cool. Cream shortening, add beaten eggs and blend well. Add sifted dry ingredients and lastly raisin mixture. Drop on greased cookie sheet and bake in moderately hot oven.

Dutch Dainties

½ cup butter
¾ cup sugar
1 tsp. baking powder

1 egg yolk and 1 whole egg
1½ cups flour
¼ tsp. salt

Combine above ingredients in the usual way. Place 1 tbsp. mixture in greased tart pans. Press with fingers to line bottom and sides. Fill each one with the following mixture:

½ cup dates and 1 cup water cooked until thick. Cool and add ⅓ cup cherries and ⅓ cup walnuts which have been chopped, 1 tsp. vanilla.

Bake in oven 375 degrees about 15 minutes. Top with whipped cream and cherry.

Jumbles

½ cup butter or shortening
1½ cups brown sugar
2 eggs, well beaten
2 cups flour

1 tsp. soda dissolved in 1 tsp. hot
   water
1 lb. dates, cut fine
½ cup chopped walnuts
½ cup crushed pineapple

Cream butter and sugar well. Add beaten eggs. Add soda, flour and fruit. Drop on greased cookie sheet and bake in moderate oven. Chopped citron or any other fruit may be added. These keep well.

June Bugs

1 tbsp. shortening
1 egg, beaten
½ cup sugar

½ cup coarsely chopped walnuts
½ cup dates, cut
1 heaping cup coconut

Cream shortening and sugar; add egg and other ingredients. Drop by teaspoonfuls on greased cookie sheet and bake 15-20 minutes in moderate oven.

Cornflake Meringues

2 egg whites
¼ tsp. cream of tartar
1 cup fine sugar
½ tsp. vanilla
¼ tsp. salt

1 cup coconut
2 cups cornflakes
1 cup dates, finely cut
¼ cup cherries, finely cut
¼ cup chopped walnuts

Beat egg whites, cream of tartar, salt, and vanilla until very stiff, but not dry. Add sugar gradually, continuing to beat after each addition. Fold in remaining ingredients and pile mixture in small mounds on well greased cookie sheet. Bake at 275 degrees for about 20 minutes.

Bachelor Buttons

1 cup brown sugar
1 cup butter (must be all
   butter)
1 cup coarsely chopped nut
   meats
1 cup coconut

½ cup glazed cherries, quartered
1 egg, unbeaten
2 cups flour
½ tsp. soda sifted with flour

Cream butter well. Add other ingredients and beat all together at one time. Drop on greased cookie sheet and bake in moderate oven.

Peanut Butter Cookies

½ cup peanut butter
½ cup shortening
½ tsp. salt
1 tsp. soda

½ cup white sugar
½ cup brown sugar
1 egg, well beaten
1⅓ cups flour
1 tsp. vanilla

Combine the first four ingredients well. Add sugar, egg, vanilla and flour. Drop from teaspoon on greased cookie sheet. Press lightly with fork to flatten. Top with peanut. Bake in moderate oven until light brown.

Peanut Butter Balls

1 cup confectioner's sugar
1 cup peanut butter
1 tsp. soft butter

½ cup chopped nut meats
½ cup chopped dates
¼ tsp. salt

Mix all ingredients together and roll the dough into small balls. Dip in plain butter icing and roll in coconut. These are not baked. Keep in cool place.

Apricot Balls

2 cups coconut
½ can condensed milk
⅔ cup chopped dried apricots

1 tsp. vanilla
½ tsp. salt

Mix ingredients, form into balls and keep in refrigerator. To improve the flavor soak apricots in liquor for several hours.

Cheese Balls

6 oz. blue cheese
8 oz. cream cheese
¼ tsp. salt

1 tbsp. pimiento
1 tbsp. chopped green pepper
dash of piquant sauce

Cream above ingredients together thoroughly and chill until easy to handle. Toast some chopped almond or walnuts watching carefully not to burn them. Form cheese mixture into balls, roll in toasted nuts and chill. Serve on board surrounded by your favorite crackers.

Cheese Straws

1 cup (packed) pastry flour
1 tsp. baking powder
3 tbsps. butter

1 cup grated cheese (cracker barrel)
1 egg yolk
2 tbsps. milk
Pinch cayenne

Sift the flour, baking powder and salt. Cut in butter, add cheese and cayenne; mix with egg yolk and milk. Roll out and cut in straws. Bake in oven 400 degrees.

Peanut Butter Fingers

2 tbsps. butter
1¼ cups confectioner's sugar
½ cup crunchy peanut butter

3 squares semi-sweet chocolate
1 cup chopped nut meats
1 tbsp. paraffin wax

Cream together the butter, sugar, peanut butter and nut meats. Form dough into fingers and chill in refrigerator for a while. Melt chocolate and wax in double boiler. Place fingers on a fork and dip in chocolate. Place on cake cooler to harden.

3-Day Cookies

3 egg whites
1 cup sugar
3 cups cornflakes, measured and rolled

½ cup all-bran
2 tbsps. flour
2 cups dates
½ cup each of cherries and nut meats

Mix altogether and beat in egg whites. Drop and bake on greased cookie sheet in moderate oven. Good in three days.

Oatmeal Cookies

1 cup butter or shortening
1 cup sugar
1 egg
2 tbsps. milk

2 cups rolled oats
1 cup flour
1 tsp. soda
1 tsp. vanilla
1 tsp. salt

Cream shortening and sugar. Add beaten egg and blend well. Add soda dissolved in milk. Add flour, oatmeal and vanilla. Roll out on canvas and cut in desired shapes. Bake in oven 350 degrees.

Variations: Cut in rounds and when cold, put together with date filling.

Mocha Cakes

Cut any butter cake or hot milk cake in small squares or oblongs. With a rolling pin crush peanuts, including a few salted ones for flavor.

Make a bowl of very thin icing and flavor to taste. With 2 forks cover piece of cake completely with frosting, take out on one fork and let drain, using second fork to scrape off drip. Drop cake pieces into a small amount of the nuts (add more when needed) covering completely or, if preferred, use grated coconut. Put cakes on a rack to harden. Icing may be put in several bowls, colored and flavored to make variety in color and flavor.

Lady Fingers

½ cup sifted confectioner's
  sugar
1 whole egg
2 egg yolks

⅓ cup cake flour
2 egg whites
⅛ tsp. salt
¼ tsp. vanilla

Fold the sugar into the stiffly beaten egg whites. Beat the whole egg and egg yolks until thick and lemon colored and fold into whites; add vanilla. Fold in carefully the flour sifted with salt. Cover baking sheet with ungreased wax paper and with a pastry tube shape lady fingers about 3 inches long and ½-inch wide. Bake in moderate oven 350 degrees for about 12 minutes.

Note: I make the batter in an 8-inch square pan and cut in fingers when cold.

Orange Squares

1 cup brown sugar
⅓ cup melted butter
1 egg, beaten
1 cup flour

1 tsp. baking powder
½ cup dates or raisins, finely cut
½ cup chopped walnuts
Juice and rind of ½ orange

Cream butter and sugar; add egg and blend well. Add juice and rind of orange, flour and baking powder sifted together, fruit and nuts. Frost with orange icing and grate a little rind on top.

Note: For special occasions loosen membrane from orange section and place sections, flower-like on top of each iced square.

Refrigerator Squares

First Layer:
2½ cups graham cracker crumbs
½ cup butter
Mix well. Bake 15 minutes at 325 degrees. Let cool.

Second Layer:
½ cup butter creamed with 1½ cups confectioner's sugar

Third Layer:
½ pint cream, whipped
1 can crushed pineapple, well drained
3 tbsps. sugar

Freeze 2 hours at coldest point. Remove from unit and keep in refrigerator.

Variation: Reserve some of the crumbs and sprinkle lightly over top of third layer. Any packaged Whip may be substituted for cream.

Heavenly Hash Squares

Cream ⅓ butter and 1 cup brown sugar

Add:

2 egg yolks	1 tsp. baking powder
1½ cups flour	1 tsp. vanilla
½ tsp. salt	

Press into pan 12 × 9 and spread over it the following mixture:

½ cup chopped cherries	½ cup coconut
½ cup chopped meats	1 cup dates, finely cut

Top with 2 egg whites beaten stiff with 1 cup brown sugar. Bake in oven 300 degrees for about 30 minutes. Cut when cool.

Caramel Squares

½ cup butter	2 cups flour
1 cup brown sugar	1 tsp. baking powder
3 egg yolks	1 tsp. vanilla

Cream butter well; add sugar and well beaten egg yolks. Add sifted dry ingredients and vanilla. Spread in pan 12 × 9. Sprinkle with 1 cup chopped nut meats and press lightly into batter. Beat the 3 egg whites until stiff; add 2 cups brown sugar gradually and pour over top. Bake in oven 350 degrees for ½ hour.

Chow Mein Drops

½ cup peanut butter
1 tin Chow mein noodles
1 pkg. chocolate or butterscotch chippets

Melt chippets in double boiler. Add noodles, peanut butter and drop on waxed paper.

Feathery Spice Squares

1 cup flour	½ cup sugar
½ tsp. salt	1 egg, beaten
3 tsps. baking powder	½ cup milk
1 tsp. cinnamon	4 tbsps. melted shortening

Sift together flour, salt, baking powder, cinnamon and sugar. Stir in the beaten egg, milk and shortening. Mix just until smooth. Pour into an 8-inch square pan, lined with wax paper, and bake in oven 425 degrees for 15 minutes.

Nut Bars

2¾ cups flour	2¼ cups brown sugar
2½ tsps. baking powder	3 eggs
½ tsp. salt	1 cup chopped nut meats
⅔ cup butter or shortening	1 6-oz. pkg. semi-sweet chocolate chips

Sift flour with baking powder and salt. Melt shortening in large saucepan, stir in brown sugar and cool slightly. Add eggs, 1 at a time, beating well after each addition. Add flour mixture, nuts and chocolate; blend well. Turn into greased pan 10½ × 15½ × ¾ inches and bake at 350 degrees for 25-30 minutes. When almost cool cut in squares. Makes approximately 48 two and one-half inch squares. Excellent for mailing.

Gelatin Marshmallow Squares

Mix and bake 10 minutes in moderate oven until light brown
(12 × 9 pan):

½ cup butter or margarine
½ cup brown sugar
1 cup flour

Stir until dissolved and boil until it threads like candy:

2 cups sugar
¾ cups boiling water

Dissolve 2 tbsps. gelatin in ½ cup cold water. Add to top mixture
and cool to lukewarm. Add 1 tsp. vanilla and ½ tsp. vinegar. Beat
until firm and divide in 2 equal parts. To 1 part add 10 cherries, cut
in pieces, and 2 tbsps. cherry juice, coloring to pale pink. To other
part add ½ cup coconut and almond flavoring. Spread pink part first
on baked mixture. Top with second part. Sprinkle with toasted
coconut. Put in refrigerator until set, and cut in squares.

Lemon Squares

10 soda crackers
½ cup butter
1 cup brown sugar

1 cup flour
1 tsp. soda
1 cup coconut

Mix together above ingredients. Line 8-inch square pan with mixture, reserving some for top. Spread with cooled lemon filling and
sprinkle with reserved mixture. Bake 15 mins. in moderate oven.

Filling:

1 lemon, grated rind and juice
2 egg yolks, beaten
1 cup sugar

3 tbsps. flour
1 cup boiling water

Cook until thick and let cool.

Chocolate Whipped Cream Squares

½ cup butter
2 tbsps. confectioner's sugar
1 cup flour

Mix together and put in 8-inch square pan. Bake 15 minutes in moderate oven. Cool.

Topping:

½ cup butter   2 eggs
⅔ cup sugar   1 tsp. vanilla
2 squares unsweetened
    chocolate, melted

Cream butter and sugar. Add chocolate and vanilla. Beat in 1 egg at a time until mixture is quite fluffy. Spread over first mixture. Spread whipped cream on top and set in refrigerator until thoroughly chilled.

Butter Rum Bars

1 pkg. (pudding included)   ⅓ cup rolled oats
    butter flavor cake mix   ½ cup butter or margarine,
1 egg   softened
½ cup chopped nuts   ½ tsp. nutmeg

Filling:

⅓ cup firmly packed brown   2 tbsps. softened margarine
    sugar   1 tsp. rum extract
1 tbsp. flour   2 eggs
1 12-oz. jar (1 cup)
    butterscotch topping

Heat oven to 375 degrees. Grease a 13 × 9 inch pan. In large bowl combine cake mix, oats, nutmeg and margarine and mix at low speed until crumbly. Reserve 1 cup crumbs for topping. To remaining crumbs blend in egg until well mixed. Press in bottom of prepared pan. Bake for 10 minutes.

In small bowl combine all filling ingredients and beat one minute at medium speed, until well mixed. Pour over crust. Sprinkle with reserved crumbs and top with nuts. Return to oven and bake 15 to 25 minutes or until golden brown. Centre will be slightly soft. Cut into bars. Yield 36 bars.

Delicious Raisin Bars

1 pkg. seeded raisins	1 tsp. cinnamon
⅓ cup shortening	½ tsp. nutmeg
1 cup brown sugar	1 tsp. ginger
1¼ cups water	¼ tsp. cloves

Boil the above ingredients for 5 minutes. Cool. Blend in 1 tsp. soda and ½ tsp. salt dissolved in 2 tsps. hot water. Add 2 cups flour sifted with 2 tsps. baking powder. Spread in buttered pan 8 × 13. Sprinkle generously with granulated sugar and bake in moderate oven 350 degrees. Cut in squares.

Variation: Omit granulated sugar and ice with 1 cup brown sugar, 3 tbsps. cream, 3 tbsps. butter and ¾ cup fine coconut boiled together for 5 minutes. Spread thinly over cake, return to oven until lightly browned.

Orange and Date Squares

½ cup butter or shortening	1 tsp. baking powder
1 cup sugar	1 cup sour milk
1 egg	1 or 2 cups dates
2 cups flour	1 tsp. soda in 1 tbsp. warm water

Cream shortening, add sugar and blend well. Add beaten egg and soda. Stir in flour alternately with milk and lastly fold in fruit and grated orange rind (1 orange). Bake in shallow pan 12 × 9 inches in oven 325 degrees for about 35 minutes. Ice as desired.

Variation: Use raisins, cherries or peel in place of dates, according to taste.

Almond Fingers

⅞ cup butter	1 tbsp. cold water
5 tbsps. sugar	1 tsp. vanilla
2 cups flour	1 cup slivered blanched almonds

Cream shortening and sugar; add vanilla. Add flour gradually, then the water and nuts. Shape into fingers and bake in oven 350 degrees for 15-20 minutes. When cool roll in white or colored granulated sugar.

Rainbow Squares

Base:

2 cups flour
1 scant cut butter

2 tbsps. sugar
¼ tsp. salt

Mix the usual way and bake about 15 minutes in oven at 350°. Let cool.

Top:

1 20-oz. tin crushed pineapple
    and juice
½ cup white sugar
3 tbsps. cornstarch

1 small bottle red cherries, sliced
1 tsp. almond flavoring
2 egg yolks

Cook until thick. Spread on baked mixture and top with meringue made with the two egg whites and ¼ cup sugar. Bake just until meringue is lightly browned.

Chocolate Chip Chews

2 cups graham wafers, rolled
    fine
1 pkg. chocolate chips
1 15-oz. tin sweetened
    condensed milk

1 tsp. vanilla
¼ cup walnuts
½ cup coconut
8 cherries, cut
¼ tsp. salt

Mix together and put into greased 8-inch square pan. Bake in oven 350 degrees for 35-40 minutes. When slightly cool, cut in squares.

Congo Bars

⅔ cup butter or shortening
1 1-lb. pkg. light brown sugar
3 eggs
2⅔ cups flour

2 tsps. baking powder
1 tsp. salt
1 pkg. chocolate bits
1 cup nut meats

Cream butter and sugar. Add eggs, 1 at a time, beating after each addition. Add vanilla and the sifted dry ingredients. Lastly add chocolate bits and nut meats. Spread on greased baking pan 13 × 9 × 1 and bake about 30 minutes in oven 375 degrees. Cut while warm.

Coconut Bars

2 eggs, beaten
1 cup (packed) brown sugar
6 tbsps. flour
1 tsp. baking powder
1 tsp. salt

1 tsp. vanilla
1½ cups coconut
¼ cup each cherries and nut
    meats

Beat eggs until thick and lemon colored; add sugar and blend well. Stir in the sifted dry ingredients, flavoring, chopped cherries, coconut and nut meats. Bake in 8-inch square pan in oven 300 degrees for 30 minutes.

Butterscotch Sticks

¼ cup butter, melted
1 cup brown sugar
1 egg, beaten
1 tsp. vanilla

½ cup coconut
1 cup flour
¼ tsp. baking powder
½ tsp. salt

Melt butter in saucepan. Stir in sugar and when dissolved remove from stove. Cool. Add beaten egg and mix well. Add the sifted dry ingredients, flavoring and coconut. Spread in 8-inch square pan and bake in moderate oven for 30 minutes. Cut in sticks when cold.

Raisin Puff Squares

2 cups flour
1 cup granulated sugar
¾ cup butter or shortening
2 eggs, slightly beaten

¼ tsp. salt
2 tsps. cream of tartar
1 tsp. baking soda
1 tsp. vanilla

Sift flour, baking soda, cream of tartar and salt. Rub in butter as for biscuits. Add sugar and eggs. Mix with hand. Roll out, the thickness of pastry, and cut in two pieces to fit pan 9 × 13 inches. Spread one piece in pan, reserving the other for top of filling. Bake until a golden brown in 350 degree oven.

Filling:

1 cup brown sugar
1 box seeded raisins
2 cups water

3 tbsps. cornstarch
1 tsp. lemon juice
⅛ tsp. salt

Cook about 10 minutes. Cool. One of my favorite squares.

Toothsome Brownies

¼ cup butter or shortening
1 cup (scant) sugar
3 eggs, beaten
½ cup flour

2 oz. unsweetened, chocolate,
　melted
½ tsp. baking powder
1 tsp. vanilla
¾ cups nuts or raisins

Cream shortening and sugar. Add eggs and mix well. Add melted chocolate, sifted flour and baking powder, vanilla and nuts. Bake at 375 degrees for about 12-15 minutes and as soon as taken from oven cover with marshmallows cut in two, placing cut side down. Ice with the following topping and when cool, cut in squares.

Icing: Melt 1 square (1 oz.) unsweetened chocolate. Add 2 tbsps. hot milk, 1 tbsp. soft butter, 1 tsp. vanilla and enough icing sugar (about 1 cup) to make of spreading consistency.

Two Layer Brownies

⅔ cup white sugar
2 eggs
⅔ cup pastry flour
½ tsp. baking powder

½ tsp. salt
1 square chocolate
½ square (⅛ lb.) butter, melted

Beat eggs until lemon colored. Add sugar beating until thick and light. Add flour, baking powder, salt, and lastly melted butter. Divide batter into two parts. To one part add ½ tsp. almond flavoring and ½ cup coconut. To other half add ½ tsp. vanilla, ¼ cup walnuts and melted chocolate. Pour white batter into 8 × 8 inch pan, then add chocolate batter. Bake in 350 degree oven. Ice with white butter peppermint icing. Dribble melted chocolate over top.

Marshmallow Squares

30 colored marshmallows
2 cups Graham Wafer crumbs
½ cup cherries
1 tin condensed milk (14 oz.)

1 tsp. vanilla
2½ cups grated coconut or less
dash of salt

Cut marshmallows in quarters and blend them with milk, crumbs, salt, vanilla, and cherries. Line 8 × 8″ pan with half the coconut. Spread the filling and press down firmly. Sprinkle remaining coconut on top and place in refrigerator for about two days.

Chocolate Fancies

½ cup butter
¼ cup sugar
3 tbsps. cocoa

1 egg, unbeaten
1 tsp. vanilla
¼ tsp. salt

Cook above ingredients in double boiler until smooth (1 or 2 minutes). Add:

2 cups graham wafer crumbs
1 cup fine coconut
½ cup chopped nut meats

Press into 9 × 12 inch pan. Mix together until creamy ¼ cup butter, 2 cups icing sugar, 2 tbsps. milk, ½ tsp. almond extract and spread on first mixture. Melt 2 squares unsweetened chocolate with 1 tbsp. butter. Cool slightly and spread over the top mixture. When chocolate is cold, cut in squares. These keep indefinitely in air tight container. Keep in refrigerator.

Cheese Squares

½ cup butter
¾ cup Velveta cheese

2 tsps. sugar
1¾ cups flour

Cream butter and cheese; mix with sugar and flour. Press ¼ of this mixture into shallow pan; cover with raspberry jam. Spread remaining crumbs on top. Bake in moderate oven. Cut in squares when cool.

Fruit Bars

½ cup soft butter
1 cup sugar
2 eggs
1 tsp. almond extract
¾ cup flour
1 tsp. baking powder
¼ tsp. salt
1 cup sliced almonds

½ cup candied cherries, halved
1 cup sliced, pitted dates
½ cup each sliced soft dried
    apricots and figs
Fine granulated sugar

Cream butter; add the 1 cup sugar and cream until fluffy. Add eggs, 1 at a time, beating well after each addition. Add sifted dry ingredients, nuts and fruit. Mix well and spread batter in a greased 9-inch square pan. Bake in oven 350 degrees for about 45 minutes. Let cool in pan. Cut in squares or bars and roll lightly in granulated sugar.

Cherry Bars

½ cup butter or shortening
½ cup sugar
2 egg yolks
½ tsp. almond extract

1½ cups flour
2 tsps. baking powder
½ tsp. salt

Cream butter and sugar well. Add beaten egg yolks and flavoring. Add the sifted dry ingredients and bake for 15 minutes in oven 350 degrees. When cool spread with lemon filling. Top with the following mixture:

2 egg whites, beaten stiff
½ cup sugar (scant)
½ tsp. vanilla

4 tbsps. chopped cherries
4 tbsps. coconut

Spread on top of lemon filling and sprinkle with chopped red and green cherries. Return to oven to brown lightly. Cut in bars or squares when cool.

Campus Squares

½ cup butter or shortening
1 cup flour

½ cup brown sugar
½ tsp. salt

Mix well and spread in pan 12 × 9. Bake for 10 minutes in oven 350 degrees. Cool. Spread on top:

2 eggs, beaten until thick and
　　lemon colored
1 cup brown sugar, added
　　gradually
3 tbsps. cocoa
1 tsp. baking powder

3 tbsps. flour
¼ tsp. salt
¾ cup nut meats or ½ cup nut
　　meats and ½ cup coconut

Bake in moderate oven. Cut when cool.

Butterscotch Squares

½ cup butter or shortening
1 cup sugar
2 eggs, separated
1 tsp. vanilla
1½ cups cake flour

½ tsp. salt
1 tsp. baking powder
1 egg white
1 cup brown sugar, firmly packed
½ cup chopped pecans

Cream shortening and sugar until fluffy. Add egg yolks, vanilla and sifted dry ingredients. Mix well and spread in a greased pan about 13 × 9 × 2. Beat egg whites stiff; gradually add brown sugar while continuing to beat. Fold in nuts and spread over mixture in pan. Bake at 350 degrees for 25 minutes. While warm cut in squares and let cool in pan.

5. Desserts, Pies and Tarts

Steamed Carrot Pudding

1 cup grated raw carrot	¾ cup seeded raisins
1 cup grated raw potato	½ cup currants
½ cup shortening or finely	¼ cup mixed peel
chopped suet	1 tsp. soda
1 cup sugar	½ tsp. cinnamon, cloves, nutmeg
1 cup flour	

Grate carrot and potato; measure and set aside. Cream shortening and sugar well; add carrot and one-half the potato and mix well. Sprinkle fruits with flour and add to mixture. Then add flour and spices which have been sifted together. Dissolve soda in remaining potato and add lastly to mixture. Mix lightly together. Pour into buttered moulds, tie down and steam for three hours. Serve with any pudding sauce.

Steamed Cranberry Pudding

3 tsps. baking soda	2 cups all-purpose flour
¾ cup boiling water	1½ tsps. baking powder
¾ cup molasses	1½ cups cranberries

Add soda to the molasses and boiling water. Sift flour with baking powder and about ¼ tsp. salt several times and combine with other mixture. Toss cranberries into the batter and stir lightly. Steam for 2 hours.

Sauce:

½ cup cream
½ cup brown sugar
¼ cup butter

Stir and cook over boiling water for 15 minutes.

Steamed Chocolate Pudding

2 cups sifted cake flour
2 tsps. baking powder
½ tsp. soda
¼ tsp. salt
½ cup sugar

⅓ cup butter or shortening
1 egg, well beaten
3 squares unsweetened chocolate,
    melted
1 cup milk

Sift flour, baking powder, soda and salt several times. Cream butter and sugar thoroughly. Add egg and chocolate; beat until smooth. Add flour alternately with milk. Steam for 2 hours. Serve with any desired sauce.

Virginia Steamed Pudding

1 cup flour
2 tsps. baking powder
1 tsp. mixed spices
1 cup sugar
1 cup shortening or suet

1 cup milk
2 eggs, beaten
1 cup bread crumbs
1 cup candied fruit

Mix same as for preceding recipe. Put into greased 2 lb. coffee or 3 lb. shortening can. Cover with wax paper or foil and tie securely with string. Put into boiling water half way up to can. When it comes to boiling point again put on low heat and steam for 2 hours. Do not uncover pan for at least one hour. Serve warm with Lemon Sauce.

Variation: Instead of fruit, fold in 1½ cups chopped dates.

Bishop Pudding

1 cup chopped apples
1 cup chopped raisins
1 cup bread crumbs

3 eggs, beaten
1 tsp. soda
Grated orange rind

Combine ingredients well and steam for 3 hours. Serve with any pudding sauce.

Baked Alaska

Baked Alaska is made by placing ice cream, frozen hard, on a piece of sponge cake and completely covering it with a meringue made by adding 2 tbsps. sugar to each beaten egg white. The cake should rest on a paper covered wet board to keep the heat out when the meringue is browned lightly in oven 425 degrees.

Snow Pudding

1 tbsp. gelatin	⅛ tsp. salt
¼ cup cold water	½ cup lemon juice
1 cup sugar	4 egg whites
1 cup boiling water	

Dissolve gelatin in cold water for 5 minutes. Add boiling water, sugar, salt and lemon juice; stir until dissolved and set in cool place until it jells, not too firm. Beat egg whites until stiff. Beat jelly mixture until foamy. Add this gradually to the egg whites, beating constantly, and continue beating until mixture is quite light and spongy. Set in refrigerator. Serve with a Soft Custard made with the egg yolks.

Snowball Dessert

1 6-oz. pkg. pineapple jello	1 cup nuts (optional)
2 9-oz. cartons "cool whip"	1 cup grated coconut
2 cups crushed pineapple	¼ tsp. salt
2 cups pineapple juice	2 tsps. vanilla
1 cup sugar	1 large Angel Food cake

Dissolve jello in 4 tbsps. ice water in large bowl. Add 1 cup boiling water; let cool. Add pineapple and pineapple juice, salt, nuts, and sugar. Let stand in refrigerator until it begins to thicken. Then add 1 carton of cool whip, vanilla, and mix well. Break cake in bite size pieces and line a 14 × 10 × 2″ pan with half the cake pieces. Spread one half of the jello mixture over cake. Put remaining cake on top and then the jello mixture. Spread the other carton of cool whip on top and sprinkle with grated coconut.

Note: For a more colorful dessert use raspberry or strawberry jello. This makes a very large dessert. Keeps well in refrigerator.

Cottage Pudding

¼ cup shortening	1¾ cups flour
1 cup sugar	½ tsp. salt
1 egg	2½ tsps. baking powder
½ tsp. lemon extract	¾ cup milk

Cream shortening and sugar thoroughly; add egg and flavoring and beat well. Add sifted dry ingredients alternately with milk, beginning and ending with flour. Bake in 8-inch square pan in oven 350 degrees for about 45 minutes. Serve warm with your favorite sauce.

Apple Knobby Pudding

1 heaping cup brown sugar
2 tbsps. shortening
1 egg, beaten
3 cups finely diced apples
½ cup chopped nuts
(optional)

1 tsp. vanilla
½ tsp. each cinnamon, nutmeg
and salt
1 tsp. soda
1 cup flour

Cream shortening, sugar and beaten egg. Add apples, nuts and vanilla; add sifted dry ingredients. Bake in oven in 350 degrees for 35-40 minutes, in an 8-inch square pan. Serve with whipped cream or Lemon Sauce.

Plum Pudding

1¼ cups flour
1 tsp. cinnamon
½ tsp. each cloves and nutmeg
¼ tsp. mace
1 tsp. salt
1½ cups stale bread crumbs
1½ cups finely grated suet
1½ cups brown sugar
1 lb. seeded raisins
1 cup seedless raisins
1 cup currants

1 cup chopped figs
1 cup chopped citron
1½ cups chopped mixed fruit
½ cup sliced blanched almonds
1 cup cherries, halved
½ cup liquid honey
4 eggs, well beaten
½ cup brandy or grape juice
½ cup milk
½ tsp. soda dissolved in 1 tbsp.
hot water

Mix ingredients in order given, sifting spices with flour. Fill well greased moulds about two-thirds full. Tie down with heavy paper or foil and steam for 6 hours. Serve piping hot with Hard Sauce.

Note: When reheating this pudding, steam for two hours.

Orange Pudding

Peel 6 oranges, remove membrane and seeds, and put into large casserole. Pour over this 1 cup sugar.

Make a custard of 3 egg yolks, 3 cups milk, ¾ cup sugar, 3 tbsps. cornstarch. Beat egg yolks well, add sugar and milk; heat in double boiler. Thicken with the cornstarch that has been mixed with a little cold milk. Cool. Pour over oranges.

Make a meringue of the 3 egg whites, beaten stiff with ⅓ cup sugar. Put this on top of custard. Sprinkle over it some grated orange rind. Put into oven to brown lightly. Chill and serve.

Lemon Pudding

Prick a lemon all over with a fork. Put into a greased casserole and add 1 cup sugar and 1 cup boiling water. On top of this put cake mix or Cottage Pudding batter. Bake as directed.

Butterscotch Pudding

1 cup brown sugar	4 slices bread
½ cup butter	½ cup milk
2 cups hot milk	1 tsp. vanilla
2 eggs, beaten	

Cook the sugar and butter until brown. Add hot milk and let stand over heat for 5 minutes. Put slices of bread into baking dish. Pour slowly over this the ½ cup milk. Mix the beaten eggs with the sugar mixture, add vanilla and pour over bread. Bake 40 minutes in a slow oven 325 degrees. Serve hot or cold with whipped cream.

Mother's Rice Pudding

3 eggs	1 cup boiled rice
1 qt. milk	½ cup raisins
¾ cup sugar (less)	Vanilla, nutmeg and salt to taste

Beat eggs; add milk and other ingredients and combine well. Put into baking dish and bake in pan of hot water at 350 degrees until set — about one hour. Stir occasionally, until it begins to set.

Lemon-Freeze

¾ cup corn flake crumbs	1 can sweetened condensed milk
2 tbsps. sugar	⅓ cup fresh lemon juice
¼ cup melted butter	½ tsp. grated lemon peel
2 eggs, separated	3 tbsps. sugar

Combine crumbs, sugar and melted butter in 8 inch pie pan or ice cube tray; mix well. Remove 2 to 4 tbsps. crumb mixture and reserve for topping. Press remaining crumb mixture evenly and firmly around sides and bottom of pan. Beat egg yolks until thick; combine with condensed milk. Add lemon juice and lemon peel; stir until thickened. Beat egg whites until stiff but not dry. Gradually beat in sugar. Fold gently into lemon mixture.

Pour into crumb lined pan; sprinkle with reserved crumbs. Freeze until firm. Cut into wedges or bars. May be garnished with fresh berries. Yield: 8 servings.

Lemon Bavarian Cream

1 tbsp. gelatin	¼ to ⅓ cup lemon juice
¼ cup cold water	3 egg whites
3 egg yolks	¼ tsp. salt
¾ cup sugar	¼ cup sugar
1 tbsp. grated lemon rind	½ pint whipping cream

Soak gelatin in cold water for 5 minutes, then dissolve over hot water. Combine egg yolks, the ¾ cup sugar, lemon rind and juice in a large bowl. Place over simmering water and beat with a rotary beater until mixture is thick and creamy, about 10 minutes. Remove from heat and beat in melted gelatin. Cool until mixture is just beginning to thicken and becomes creamy. Make a meringue of the egg whites, salt and remaining ¼ cup sugar. Fold into the gelatin mixture, then fold in the stiffly beaten cream. Pour mixture into a 5 to 6 cup serving dish and chill until set. Just before serving decorate with whipped cream, slivered toasted almonds and pieces of maraschino cherry. 6 to 8 servings.

Pineapple Upside Down Cake

1 cup sugar	1⅓ tsps. baking powder
3 eggs	½ cup cold water
1½ cups cake flour	1 tsp. lemon flavoring

Cover bottom of a 9-inch square pan with brown sugar. Pour over it ⅓ cup melted butter. Arrange slices of drained pineapple on top (crushed may be used, if well drained). A few red cherries may be added.

Make cake batter. Beat eggs well; add sugar gradually. Add the sifted dry ingredients alternately with cold water. Add flavoring and pour batter over fruit. Bake in oven 350 degrees for 40-45 minutes. Top with whipped cream.

Apple Upside Down Cake

¼ cup shortening	1 tsp. baking powder
3 tbsps. sugar	½ tsp. soda
1 egg, beaten	1 tsp. ginger
⅓ cup molasses	½ tsp. cinnamon
1 cup less 2 tbsps. flour	¼ tsp. salt
	⅓ cup boiling water

Cover bottom of an 8-inch square baking dish with ⅓ cup brown sugar. Pour over it ⅓ cup melted butter. Add 1 tbsp. lemon juice and cook for a few minutes. Pare and core 3 large apples; cut crosswise in half. Arrange rings on top of sugar mixture in pan.

Make batter. Cream shortening and sugar; add egg and molasses. Sift together other ingredients and add to batter. Lastly add boiling water, mixing quickly. Spread batter over apples and bake in oven 350 degrees for about 40 minutes. Serve with whipped cream.

Delicious Strawberry Squares

Bottom Layer
¾ cup cornflake crumbs
2 tbsp. sugar
¼ cup melted butter

Mix well and spread on bottom of 8 × 8 inch pan, reserving about 3 tbsps. for top. Bake in moderate oven about 10 min.

Top Layer
Boil 1 pkg. frozen strawberries for one minute. Add
1 pkg. strawberry jello
½ cup sugar
Juice of 1 lemon

Cool mixture until it starts to thicken. Add ½ cup cream, whipped. Pour over bottom layer. Whip another ½ cup cream and spread on top. Sprinkle with crumbs. Keep in refrigerator.

Jiffy Pudding

½ cup sugar
1 cup flour
1 tsp. baking powder

1 cup raisins, berries or rhubarb
½ cup milk
¼ tsp. salt
½ tsp. vanilla

To the sifted dry ingredients add the sugar and raisins. Add vanilla to milk and mix quickly.

Sauce: 1 cup brown sugar, 2 cups boiling water, butter the size of an egg. Bring to a boil; put into large casserole and put the first mixture on top. Bake in moderate oven 375 degrees about 45 minutes.

For a chocolate sauce, omit the nutmeg and raisins and add 1 cup chocolate chips.

Strawberry, Raspberry or Peach Shortcake Biscuit Recipe:

2 cups sifted flour
4 tsps. baking powder
1 tsp. salt

5 tbsps. shortening
¾ cup rich milk or cream

Sift dry ingredients. Cut in butter until like coarse crumbs. Add milk and combine with a few swift strokes. Handle dough as little as possible. Pat dough ½ inch thick and cut with a large floured biscuit cutter. Bake in hot oven 450 degrees for about 15 minutes. Split; spread sweetened fruit between layers, and on top. Garnish with whipped cream. Top with a few large strawberries dipped in sugar.

Sponge Cake Recipe:

1 cup sifted flour
1 tsp. baking powder
¼ tsp. salt
⅞ cup sugar

3 eggs, slightly beaten
3 tbsps. cold water
1 tsp. vanilla

Sift dry ingredients into mixing bowl. Make a well in center and place in it the beaten eggs, water and flavoring; beat until smooth. Pour into a 10-inch layer pan and bake at 350 degrees for 20-25 minutes. Spread cake with sweetened fruit and top with whipped cream or cut in squares for individual servings and decorate as directed.

Raspberry Bavarian

1 package (15 oz.) frozen
    raspberries
2 tablespoons cornstarch
1 envelope gelatin
1 tbsp. lemon juice
½ cup granulated sugar

¼ tsp. salt
2 eggs separated
½ cup creám
1 9-inch baked, coconut
    meringue shell

Drain raspberries reserving ¾ cup of juice. In top of double boiler blend juice with corn starch; mix in gelatin, lemon juice, ¼ cup sugar, salt and 2 egg yolks. Cook mixture over boiling water, stirring constantly until mixture thickens. Remove from heat and fold in raspberries. Cool until consistency of egg white. Beat egg whites to form stiff peaks; gradually beat in remaining ¼ cup of sugar until mixture is stiff and shiny. Whip cream until stiff. Fold meringue and cream into raspberry mixture. Turn into baked, cooled 9-inch coconut meringue pie shell. Chill until firm.

To use fresh raspberries, sprinkle the raspberries with ¼ cup sugar and 1 tablespoon lemon juice as called for in recipe. Allow to stand for 30 minutes, measure juice and add sufficient water to make ¾ cup. Proceed as recipe directs.

Apple Dumplings

Make a syrup by boiling together 1 cup sugar, 2 cups water, 2 tbsps. butter and ¼ tsp. cinnamon or nutmeg.

Roll out pastry and cut in about 6-inch squares. Pare and core a medium tart apple for each square. Place apple on each square of pastry. Fill each apple cavity with cinnamon and sugar. (½ cup sugar and 1 tsp. cinnamon sufficient for 6 dumplings). Dot with butter. Bring opposite points of pastry up over the apple; moisten with milk and seal. Place apart on baking dish and cover with the prepared syrup. Bake for about 45 minutes in oven 375 degrees. Serve with syrup and cream.

Variation: Use sliced apples instead of whole apple. When making pastry add some grated cheese to make the dumplings extra good.

Apple Crisp

Slice 12 large apples, peeled and cored, into a bowl and mix with ½ cup sugar, 2 tsps. lemon juice, ½ tsp. cinnamon, ¼ tsp. ground cloves. Transfer the apple mixture to a well buttered 3-quart baking dish.

Topping:

Combine ¾ cup sifted flour, ½ cup sugar, ⅛ tsp. salt. Cut in 6 tbsps. butter until mixture is crumbly. Stir in ¼ cup chopped nuts and sprinkle the mixture over the apples. Bake in moderate oven at 350° for 45 minutes or until apples are tender and topping is brown. Serve plain or topped with whipped cream or ice cream.

Quick Gingerbread

3 eggs
1 cup white sugar
1 cup molasses
1 tsp. each cloves, ginger,
    cinnamon, salt

1 cup salad oil
$2\frac{1}{8}$ cups all-purpose flour
2 tsps. baking soda dissolved in
    $\frac{1}{8}$ cup warm water
1 cup hot water

Put eggs, sugar, molasses, spices, salt, and oil in large electric mixer bowl and beat well. Sift in flour and beat until fluffy. Dissolve soda in warm water; add to the mixture and mix well. Lastly add the hot water and beat lightly and quickly. Pour into 9 × 13 inch pan and bake in 350 degree oven. Serve hot with whipped cream. This is a prize recipe!

Variations: Bake gingerbread in layer cake pans for about 25 minutes. As soon as removed from oven, spread top of one layer with sliced marshmallows. Place the other cake layer on top and return to oven for 3 minutes longer. Serve hot with whipped cream.

When blueberries are in season, add to batter 1 cup berries dredged with 1 tbsp. flour.

Split gingerbread squares and spread with the following cheese-fruit mixture, sandwich style: Combine $\frac{1}{2}$ cup drained crushed pineapple with 3 ounces cream cheese. Add $\frac{1}{4}$ cup chopped pecans or any other nut meats. Top with whipped cream and sprinkle lightly with crystallized ginger.

Molasses Apple Pudding

1 cup flour
2 tsps. baking powder
$\frac{1}{4}$ tsp. salt

1 tbsp. butter or shortening
$\frac{1}{3}$ cup milk or enough milk to
    make as for biscuits

Prepare above ingredients as for Biscuits. Roll out as for jelly roll. Spread with chopped or sliced apples, raisins, cinnamon and sprinkle over this a wee bit of brown sugar. Roll up, sealing ends. In a separate bowl mix $\frac{3}{4}$ cup molasses, 1 cup water and 1 heaping tbsp. butter. Put roll into large baking dish and pour mixture over it, allowing mixture to go around roll. Bake, basting frequently, in oven 350 degrees. Serve with light cream.

Blueberry or Apple Grunt

1 quart blueberries
½ cup sugar
⅔ cup water

Put ingredients into saucepan and bring to boiling point. Sift together 2 cups flour, 2 tsps. baking powder and ¼ tsp. salt. Cut in 1 tbsp. butter or shortening and add enough milk (about ⅔ cup) to make a soft biscuit dough. Drop by spoonfuls in the hot berries. Cover tightly and cook 12-15 minutes. Do not lift cover while cooking.

Make **Apple Grunt** the same way, using thinly sliced apples in place of the berries and add ¼ tsp. grated nutmeg and 1 tsp. lemon juice. Cook apples until tender before adding batter.

Baked Custard

2 eggs   ⅛ tsp. salt
2 cups milk, scalded   Vanilla flavoring
2 to 4 tbsps. sugar (to taste) Coconut

Beat eggs well; add sugar, salt and flavoring. Add hot milk gradually and combine well. Pour into buttered large or individual moulds. Bake, in a pan of hot water, in oven 325 degrees, until custard is firm. Custard is done when a knife inserted comes out clean. Serve plain, with whipped cream, or make a meringue of 1 egg white and 1 tsp. sugar and arrange roughly on top. Sprinkle with a little grated coconut and return to oven to brown lightly.

Variation: Line bottom and sides of baking dish with Lady Fingers or Sponge Cake, cut in pieces. Place a layer of well drained fruit or jam in bottom of pan and over this pour the custard mixture which has been previously cooked until thick, and cooled slightly. Top with meringue and bake in slow oven until meringue is set.

Orange Sponge Dessert

Grease cake pan and put in light sponge cake. Sprinkle liberally over it fresh orange juice and cover with the chopped fresh orange. I use 2 large oranges. Cover with a custard sauce and over this a topping of meringue. Brown in oven.

Baked Grapefruit

Prepare as for breakfast. Top with brown sugar and butter. Heat in oven until butter and sugar are melted and blended with fruit.

Lemon Grapenut Pudding

¼ cup butter
¾ cup sugar
2 eggs, separated
Pinch of salt

2 tbsps. flour
3 tbsps. grapenuts
1 cup milk
⅓ cup lemon juice

Cream butter; add sugar, flour and salt, blending well. Add beaten egg yolks, then milk, grapenuts, and juice. Lastly fold in the beaten egg whites. Pour into buttered casserole, place in pan of hot water and bake in oven 325 degrees for about 1 hour.

Chocolate Whipped Cream

1 pt. milk
4 tbsps. sugar
2 squares unsweeteend
    chocolate

2 tbsps. cornstarch
1 cup whipped cream

Cook together in top of double boiler the milk, sugar and chocolate until chocolate is dissolved, stirring frequently. Stir in cornstarch dissolved in ⅓ cup water or milk and cook until it thickens. Set aside to cool. Just before serving beat up chocolate mixture with a spoon. Fold in the whipped cream to which has been added 2 tbsps. confectioner's sugar and a little vanilla. Serve in sherbet glasses. This makes a delicious dessert.

Burnt Almond Freeze

½ cup sugar
½ cup boiling water
1 tsp. unflavored gelatin
1 tbsp. cold water

1½ cups heavy cream
1 tsp. vanilla
¼ cup blanched almonds

Put ¼ cup of the sugar into saucepan and cook over medium heat, stirring constantly, until sugar turns a caramel color. Remove from stove and cool for 3 minutes. Add the boiling water and cook over low heat for several minutes. Sprinkle gelatin over cold water to soften. Stir gelatin and the ½ cup cream into syrup and cool until thick. Whip until stiff the remaining cream (1 cup). Add the other ¼ cup sugar and flavoring. Fold into the thickened syrup mixture and freeze in refrigerator tray, until mushy. Put almonds in oven and brown to a rich golden color; chop coarsely and beat into the mushy mixture, for several minutes. Pour into freezing tray and freeze. Serves 8.

Orange Delight

Dissolve 1 level tbsp. gelatin in ¼ cup cold water for 5 minutes. Add ¾ cup boiling water, ½ cup orange juice, 1 tbsp. lemon juice, ½ cup sugar, pinch of salt and grated rind of 1 orange.

Beat all ingredients with egg beater until mixed. Cool, and when set, not too firm, give it a few twirls with egg beater. Fold in ½ cup cream, whipped. Keep in refrigerator but do not freeze.

Rice Delight

Whip 1 cup, or less, heavy cream; add 3 tbsps. sugar, about 8 quartered marshmallows, ½ cup diced well drained pineapple, and a few chopped toasted almonds (optional). Fold in lightly 1½ cups cooked chilled rice. Pile lightly in sherbet glasses.

Cream Puffs

½ cup butter
1 cup boiling water
1 cup flour

¼ tsp. salt
3 large or 4 small eggs

Melt butter in water; add flour and salt all at once, and stir vigorously. Cook, stirring constantly, until it leaves the sides of pan and forms a ball. Remove from fire; add unbeaten eggs, one at a time, beating well after each addition. Drop from tablespoon on greased baking dish about 2 inches apart, heaping mixture in the center. Bake in preheated oven 400 degrees for about 30 minutes, reducing heat to 300 degrees for another 20 minutes. Cut off tops with sharp knife, fill and replace tops. Keep any extra puffs in cold place in air tight container and fill when needed.

Rich Custard Filling: Mix together in saucepan ½ cup sugar, ½ tsp. salt, ⅓ cup flour. Stir in 2 cups milk and let come to a boil slowly, stirring constantly. Boil for 1 minute. Remove from heat and stir a little hot mixture into 2 beaten eggs. Return to saucepan and heat just to boiling point. When cold, add flavoring.

Whipped Cream Filling: Add a little sugar and flavoring to heavy whipped cream. Fruit may be added or puffs may be filled with ice cream.

Tiny Puffs or Eclairs: Drop mixture by small spoonfuls and fill with chicken salad or any desired mixture.

Pear Delight

Spread pears, canned or fresh, with fresh cranberry sauce; cover with foil and bake until tender. Chill, top with sweetened whipped cream, and coconut plain or toasted.

Griddle Cakes

1½ cups sour milk	1 tbsp. sugar
1 tsp. soda stirred into milk	2 eggs, separated and well beaten
½ tsp. salt	Flour

Mix the first four ingredients; add beaten egg yolks and enough flour to stiffen (about 2 cups). Fold mixture slowly into the stiffly beaten egg whites. Batter may be made in advance and kept in refrigerator. Serve with Sunshine Sauce, or Amber Syrup.

Calla Lilies

Beat until thick and light 1 egg and a few grains of salt. Beat in gradually ¼ cup sugar, and 1 tsp. vanilla or any other flavoring. Fold in alternately 6 tbsps. flour and 1½ tsps. cold water. Drop batter in small mounds on greased baking sheet, having no more than 5 or 6 mounds on each sheet, and with a spoon spread each mound into a round, about 4 inches in diameter. Bake in preheated oven 375 degrees, just to a light golden color — about 5 minutes. Working at the open oven, loosen one at a time, turn upside down and shape into a cone. Place on cake cooler and when cold and ready to serve fill with whipped cream, sweetened and flavored. Dot with jelly to resemble calla lily bloom.

Variation: When mounds are spread out, just before putting into oven, spread with finely chopped nuts or coconut. To vary the filling add some powdered instant coffee.

Lemon Chiffon Dessert

Line a 9 × 12 inch cake pan with wax paper. Into this put ice cream wafer crumbs, crushed fine or put through food chopper. Use 2 packages, reserving ½ package for top.

1 large can chilled evaporated milk	¾ cup (less) sugar
	⅛ tsp. salt
1 pkg. lemon jello	1 lemon, juice and rind

Dissolve jello in ¼ cup boiling water, add sugar and stir well; add lemon juice and rind. Cool until it begins to set. Whip chilled milk until thick and fold into jello mixture. Put this over crumbs and sprinkle remaining crumbs over top. Chill for several hours in refrigerator. Cut in squares, serve with whipped cream, and decorate with cherry.

Raspberry Torte

1 pkg. frozen raspberries	Raspberry syrup and water to
2 tbsps. unflavored gelatin	make 1 cup
½ cup water	1 cup heavy cream, whipped
	Angel Cake, Sponge Cake or
	Lady Fingers

Soften gelatin in water; dissolve in hot raspberry syrup. Chill until almost set; beat until fluffy.

Fold in whipped cream; add berries.

Line angel cake pan with cake or lady fingers; pour in one-half mixture. Place additional cake pieces in the center and pour in remaining mixture; chill.

Note: This dessert is better if made a day before serving.

Chocolate Charlotte

1 envelope unflavored gelatin	1 tsp. vanilla
¾ cup sugar	1 tsp. cinnamon
½ tsp. salt	4 eggs, separated
3 squares unsweetened	1 cup heavy cream
chocolate	½ cup slivered almonds
1½ cups milk	12 lady fingers

Mix gelatin, sugar and salt; add chocolate, milk, and heat until chocolate melts. Beat smooth.

Beat egg yolks; stir in part of hot chocolate mixture and cook until thick. Add vanilla and cinnamon. Chill until it begins to freeze. Beat egg whites and cream until stiff. Beat gelatin mixture until fluffy. Fold in egg whites, cream and almonds. Line angel cake pan with lady fingers. Pour in one-half mixture; arrange more lady fingers in center and pour in remaining mixture. Chill until firm. Top with whipped cream. (Better made the day before serving).

Pineapple Charlotte

2 tbsps. unflavored gelatin
½ cup cold water
3 egg yolks
2 cups milk
1 cup sugar

3 egg whites, beaten
1 cup cream
1 can crushed pineapple, drained
½ cup finely chopped nuts
Angel Cake, broken in pieces

Soften gelatin in cold water. Beat egg yolks; add milk and sugar. Cook over hot water until mixture coats spoon. Add gelatin and stir until dissolved. Cool. Add pineapple, fold in stiffly beaten cream and egg whites, nuts. Line pan with cake and pour in one-half the mixture; add more cake and remaining mixture.

Trifle

Thaw 1 package of frozen raspberries. Prepare custard and let cool. Cut sponge cake or any stale white cake in cubes. Into a large bowl put a layer of the prepared cake. Spread over it a layer of raspberries, using about 4 tsps. of the juice for each layer. Cover with custard and over this sprinkle a little sherry or Madeira. Continue to fill bowl with alternate layers, as instructed, ending with custard. Chill for several hours. Before serving cover with whipped cream. Using a pastry bag with a fluted tube pipe rosettes of whipped cream on top. Sprinkle with toasted slivered almonds or whole raspberries.

Custard:

6 tbsps. flour
1 cup sugar
⅛ tsp. salt

4 eggs
4 cups milk, scalded
2 tsps. vanilla

Mix flour, sugar and salt. Add the slightly beaten eggs. Gradually add the milk. Cook over hot water, stirring constantly, until mixture thickens and coats the spoon. Remove from heat and let cool. A truly exquisite dessert for buffet or special occasion.

Quick Bread Pudding

Grease double boiler. Put in 1 cup brown sugar, 3 or 4 slices of buttered bread, cut in cubes. Beat 3 eggs; add 2 cups milk, ¼ tsp. salt and ½ tsp. vanilla. Put on top of bread and steam for 1½ hours.

Meringue Glacé

Preheat oven to 250 degrees.

Beat to soft peaks 4 egg whites, ¼ tsp. cream of tartar. Gradually beat in 1 cup fine granulated sugar. Beat until the sugar dissolves and the meringue is stiff and glossy. Do not overbeat. Fold in ½ tsp. vanilla. Cover baking sheets with brown paper. I draw the outline (rounds) of desired size on the brown paper and shape the meringues to fit, making them a uniform size. For each shell, drop about ⅓ cup meringue onto the brown paper, keeping them well apart. A pastry tube is excellent for shaping the shells. Bake in oven 250 degrees for 1 hour. Turn off heat and leave meringues in the oven, door ajar, until cooled. Yield: 12 meringues. Fill with ice cream and top with chocolate sauce.

Variation: Heat 1 cup red currant jelly slowly with 1 tbsp. cognac for an elegant topping.

Shredded Wheat Pudding

1 shredded wheat biscuit
1 egg
1 pt. milk

½ cup brown sugar or ¼ cup molasses
½ tsp. salt
Raisins (optional)

Break up biscuit into bottom of baking dish. Mix the other ingredients and pour over it. Bake about 35 minutes in moderate oven 350 degrees. Serve warm with whipped cream or ice cream.

Snappy Pumpkin Pudding

Fill custard cups with some of the pumpkin mixture prepared as for pies. Use canned or fresh pumpkin. Place a gingersnap on top of each custard dish. Bake, and served with whipped cream.

Orange Ice Cream Dessert

2 pkgs. orange jello
1 10-oz can Mandarin oranges
1 pint vanilla ice cream

1 cup whipping cream, whipped
½ cup juice from oranges

Fill cup measure with boiling water (½ juice, ½ water). Into this liquid dissolve jello thoroughly. Stir in the ice cream, oranges, and whipped cream. Pour into dish and keep in refrigerator. Best made a day in advance.

Pineapple Ice Cream Dessert

2 pkgs. pineapple jello　　　1 pint vanilla ice cream
1 cup boiling water　　　　　1 cup cream, whipped
1 19-oz tin crushed pineapple,
　　halved, and using half
　　the juice

Dissolve jello in boiling water and let set until cooled. Beat with beater, add pineapple, ice cream and whipped cream. Keep in refrigerator. Best made a day in advance.

Note: These two puddings are delicious and a memorable ending to any meal.

Superb Pastry

5 cups flour　　　　　1 egg
2 tsps. salt　　　　　1 tbsp. vinegar
1 lb. shortening　　　water

Sift well the flour and salt. Cut in shortening with pastry blender until mixture resembles a very coarse meal. Put egg in cup, add vinegar and fill cup with water. Add gradually to mixture, mixing only enough to hold together. Press in roll and wrap in buttered wax paper. This keeps indefinitely in refrigerator. When taking pastry from refrigerator, before rolling out, allow it to come to room temperature. Pastry you will be proud to serve.

Flaky Pastry

Make same as for Plain Pastry, but add to flour mixture $\frac{1}{4}$ tsp. baking powder and decrease shortening $\frac{1}{4}$ cup. When dough is rolled out, as instructed, use an extra $\frac{1}{4}$ cup butter as follows: Dot over with $\frac{1}{3}$ of the butter; roll up like jelly roll, pat roll flat on the top with rolling pin, repeating this until all the butter is used. Chill thoroughly.

Hot Water Pastry

$\frac{1}{3}$ cup boiling water　　　2 cups flour
$\frac{2}{3}$ cup shortening　　　　$\frac{3}{4}$ tsp. salt

Pour water over shortening; beat until creamy. Cool. Add flour and salt sifted together and mix with fork, to soft dough. Wrap in wax paper and chill thoroughly before rolling. This is sufficient pastry for one 8-inch double crust pie.

Pastry for Tarts

Follow recipe for Hot Water Pastry but substitute lemon juice for one-half the water and add grated lemon or orange rind and egg yolk.

Favorite Crumb Crust

Mix well 1 cup graham cracker crumbs, ½ cup crushed corn flakes, ⅓ cup sugar and ½ cup melted butter. Press firmly into a 9-inch pie plate. Do not over bake.

Note: When making a pie shell, prick the entire surface with a fork and bake in a hot oven 400 degrees for 12 minutes. Do not prick shell if filling is to be baked in it.

Apple Pie

Line a 9 inch pie plate with pastry. Wash, core and cut in very thin slices about 6 medium-sized unpeeled tart apples (the peeling gives added color and flavor). Sprinkle over the top about 1 small cup white sugar, depending on the tartness of the apples, ¼ tsp. grated nutmeg and 1 tsp. lemon juice. Dot with butter. Cover the pie with an upper crust which has slits cut in it. Seal and flute edge. Bake in oven 450 degrees for 10 minutes, decreasing heat to 325 degrees and bake until nicely browned and apples are tender. Allow about 1 hour for the baking.

Dutch Apple Pie

Line a 9-inch pie plate with pastry. Put in 3 cups pared sliced apples. Mix together 1 cup sugar, ½ tsp. cinnamon, 3 tbsps. flour. Beat 1 egg, add 1 cup light cream, 1 tsp. vanilla, and blend well with sugar mixture. Pour this over the apples and sprinkle with some finely chopped nuts. Dot with butter and bake in moderate oven 375 degrees until apples are tender. As soon as removing pie from oven sprinkle with shredded cheese. This pie is best when served warm.

Open-Faced Apple Pie

Make as for Apple Pie but omit top crust. It may be topped with whipped cream; grated cheese, and then put under the broiler to melt, or with the following mixture put on before baking the pie: Melt 6 tbsps. butter. Stir in 1 cup fine dry bread or Zwieback crumbs, ½ tsp. cinnamon, and brown lightly.

Apple Amber Pie

1 unbaked pie shell
1½ lbs. apples, pared and
    sliced
½ cup white sugar

A little water
2 or 3 eggs
¼ cup butter

Stew the apples in water, sugar and butter, adding just enough water to cook apples. Mash with a fork. Add the beaten egg yolks and pour into lined pie plate. Bake in a moderately hot oven 375 degrees until the pastry is done and the filling is firm. Beat the egg whites to a stiff froth, fold in 2 tbsps. powdered or granulated sugar, spread on pie and return to oven to brown lightly.

Deep Dish Apple Pie

Bake in pastry lined 6½ × 10½-inch oblong baking dish, or fill with apple filling, and put pastry on top.

Pumpkin or Squash Pie

1 cup cooked pumpkin or
    squash
½ cup brown sugar
3 tbsps. molasses or corn syrup
2 eggs
1½ cups milk
½ tsp. ginger

1 tbsp. melted butter
½ tsp. salt
Lemon, vanilla extract
¼ tsp. grated nutmeg
Cinnamon to taste (optional)

Mix pumpkin or squash with sugar, molasses, spices and melted butter. Add milk and beaten eggs and mix thoroughly. Pour into 9-inch unbaked pie shell and bake for 10 minutes in oven preheated to 475 degrees. Decrease heat to 325 degrees and continue baking until filling is set.

Note: A little cinnamon sprinkled over the top of filling before putting pie into oven is quite desirable, or pie may be garnished with whipped cream to which has been added tiny pieces of candied ginger.

Pumpkin Chiffon Pie

Separate three large eggs, putting whites in one bowl and yolks in another. To the yolks add 1 cup brown sugar, ½ tsp. salt, ¼ tsp. nutmeg, ½ tsp. (or less) cinnamon. 1½ cups canned pumpkin. Stir well. Heat 1 cup milk to scalding point. Stir into above mixture. Beat egg whites until stiff and gently fold into the pumpkin mixture. Pour into a large pie shell which has been baked for 10 mins. at 425° and bake for another 10 minutes at same temperature. Reduce heat to 350° and bake for one hour. Serve topped with whipped cream. Excellent.

Buttermilk Pie

2 eggs
1 cup sugar
2 tbsps. flour

2 cups buttermilk
2 tbsps. butter, melted

Mix together the sugar and flour and add gradually to the well beaten eggs. Add buttermilk and butter. Mix well. Pour into unbaked pastry lined 9-inch pie plate and bake for 10 minutes in oven 475 degrees, lowering heat to 325 degrees to complete baking.

Rhubarb Strawberry Pie

Line pie plate with pastry. Wash, dry and cut up sufficient rhubarb to fill plate, about 4 cups. Sprinkle over this 1½ cups sugar and 1 tbsp. flour. In season, put a layer of sliced strawberries over rhubarb, or strawberry jam may be used but decrease the amount of sugar when using jam. Cover with pastry, and bake as for Apple Pie, allowing same time so that the filling will thicken.

One Crust Rhubarb Pie

2 cups unpeeled rhubarb,
    diced
2 egg yolks

1 cup sugar
2 tsps. flour

Pour boiling water over rhubarb and let stand for 5 minutes. Drain well. Add egg yolks, sugar and flour to rhubarb and fill unbaked pie shell. Bake until custard has set. Make a meringue with the egg whites and ½ cup white sugar. Add a little lemon flavoring and brown lightly in oven.

Berry Pies

Line pie plate with pastry. Fill with strawberries, blueberries, huckleberries or any other fruit. Sprinkle on top of fruit 1 cup sugar, ⅛ tsp. salt, and about 2 tbsps. flour. Bake as for Apple Pie. For berry pies add sugar according to the acidity of the fruit. If berries are very ripe, add 1 to 2 tbsps. lemon juice for tartness.

Lemon Meringue Pie

1 cup sugar
5 tbsps. cornstarch
⅛ tsp. salt
2 cups water
3 egg yolks, beaten

2 tbsps. butter
⅓ cup lemon juice
2 tsps. grated lemon rind
3 egg whites
⅛ tsp. salt
2 tbsps. powdered sugar

Cook sugar, cornstarch, salt and water over low heat until mixture thickens and boils. Cook, covered, for 10 minutes longer. Pour a little of this over the beaten egg yolks and then add it ot the mixture in the double boiler. Cook and stir the custard about 3 minutes longer. Remove from heat. Beat in butter, lemon juice and rind. Cool slightly and pour into a 9-inch baked pie shell. Cover with meringue made with egg whites, salt, and powdered sugar. Put into oven and brown lightly.

Variation: To the above filling add the juice of half an orange and a little grated rind. Fold 1 stiffly beaten egg white into filling and use the whites of the other two for meringue. Add about 8 quartered marshmallows to slightly cooled filling before pouring into pie crust.

Lime Pie

Use juice and rind of lime instead of lemon. Omit butter. Add a few drops of green food coloring to enhance the color.

Lemon Sponge Pie

1 cup sugar
1½ tsps. butter
2 tbsps. flour
2 eggs, separated

Pinch salt
1 cup sweet milk
Juice and rind of lemon

Cream butter and sugar. Add slightly beaten egg yolks, flour, salt, milk, juice and rind of lemon. Lastly fold in the stiffly beaten egg whites. Put into unbaked pie shell and bake in oven 450 degrees for the first 10 minutes, lowering heat to 350 degrees until filling is set.

Raisin Pie

1 cup seedless raisins
1 cup water
2 tbsps. butter
½ cup sugar
2 tbsps. flour

2 egg yolks, slightly beaten
1 tsp. grated lemon or orange
rind
3 tbsps. lemon juice
2 eggs whites

Cook raisins and water to the boiling point; add sugar. Cool half a cupful of this mixture and to it add the butter and flour. Return to saucepan and cook over low heat until thickened. Remove from fire and add egg yolks, rind and juice of lemon. Fill baked pie shell and use the egg whites and 2 or 3 tbsps. powdered sugar to make a meringue for topping, or put filling between two crusts and bake at 450 degrees for 10 minutes, decreasing heat to 350 degrees until done.

Pineapple Fluff Pie

2½ tbsps. cornstarch
½ cup water
1 cup pineapple juice
¾ cup sugar
1 cup drained crushed
pineapple

3 egg whites
¼ tsp. salt
1 baked pie shell
Whipped cream

Blend cornstarch and water. Add pineapple juice, ½ cup sugar and cook slowly until thickened, stirring constantly. Add pineapple and cook a few minutes longer. Combine egg whites and salt and beat until foamy; add remaining sugar gradually, beating until stiff. Fold into pineapple mixture and pour into pie shell. Cool. Spread with whipped cream. Makes one 9-inch pie.

Custard Pie

4 eggs
½ cup sugar
¼ tsp. salt

¼ tsp. nutmeg
1 tsp. vanilla
2 cups warm milk

Beat eggs well and combine with sugar, salt, nutmeg and vanilla. Add milk (do not scald) slowly; mix well and pour into a 9-inch pastry lined pie plate. Bake in oven 450 degrees for 10 minutes, decreasing heat to 325 degrees for about 25 minutes longer. Do not over bake as this causes custard to become watery.

Pecan Pie

3 eggs
¾ cup sugar
⅓ tsp. salt

⅓ cup melted butter
1 cup dark corn syrup
1 cup pecans, sliced

Beat eggs well and add other ingredients. Mix well and pour into pie shell. Bake for the first 10 minutes at 425 degrees and finish baking at 375 degrees for about 30-35 minutes.

Mock Pecan Pie

⅔ cup uncooked oatmeal
¾ cup light corn syrup
2 eggs, well beaten
¾ cup sugar

1 tsp. vanilla
¾ cup melted butter, cooled
1 unbaked pie shell

Preheat oven to 350°. Mix all ingredients in the order listed. Pour into pie shell and bake for 1 hour. Top with whole or chopped pecans, if preferred. Makes a delicious pie.

Strawberry Angel Pie

18 marshmallows
2 tbsps. crushed fresh
   strawberries
2 egg whites, stiffly beaten
¼ cup sugar

¼ tsp. salt
1 pint firm vanilla ice cream
1 cup fresh sliced strawberries
1 baked pie shell

Put marshmallows and crushed strawberries into saucepan. Place over low heat. Stir until marshmallows are melted. Beat sugar gradually into stiffly beaten egg whites. Add salt. Gradually beat in cooked marshmallow mixture. Fill pastry shell with the ice cream. Spread over it the sliced strawberries, and top with swirls of marshmallow meringue, being sure to completely cover ice cream. Brown quickly under broiler and serve immediately.

Strawberry Surprise Pie

1 baked pastry shell	3 egg whites
3½ cups strawberries	¾ cup white sugar
½ cup powdered sugar	Ice cream

Prepare strawberries and sprinkle with the powdered sugar. Let stand and make meringue by beating the egg whites very stiff and adding the white sugar. Place in shell a layer of strawberries, a layer of very hard ice cream and a second layer of berries, and finally the meringue. The meringue must carefully seal in every bit of the ice cream and fruit. Brown lightly under the broiler and serve at once.

Cream Pie

3 egg yolks	1 tbsp. butter
⅓ cup sugar	2 cups warm milk
¼ tsp. salt	¼ tsp. grated nutmeg
2½ tbsps. cornstarch	2 egg whites

Beat egg yolks well. Beat in gradually the sugar, salt, cornstarch and melted butter. Pour over these ingredients the warm milk. Cook in top of double boiler, or over very low heat, until it thickens. Cool and add flavoring. Put into baked shell. Cover with meringue made of the egg whites, 3 tbsps. icing sugar and ⅛ tsp. salt. Bake in a slow oven until lightly browned. Instead of the meringue, a ring of whipped cream sprinkled with grated coconut may be placed around the pie.

Variations of Cream Filling:

Coconut Cream Filling: When filling is cooked stir in ½ cup shredded coconut.

Orange Coconut Filling: Follow Cream Pie recipe but add 1 extra tbsp. cornstarch. Add to the cooled filling 1 whole finely ground orange (remove seeds). Top meringue with orange flavored coconut made by rubbing coconut and orange gratings together until the coconut takes on an orange flavor and color.

Caramel Filling: Caramelize ¼ cup of the sugar in basic recipe. Gradually add milk and other ingredients. Bake as directed.

Pineapple Filling: Add ½ cup thoroughly drained crushed pineapple to cooled filling.

Banana Cream Filling: Slice 2 bananas in baked pie shell. Pour over bananas the cream filling. Top with meringue or whipped cream and a few slices of banana on top when ready to serve.

Chocolate Cream Filling: Cut up 1 square chocolate and put into double boiler with the cold milk. Heat until chocolate is melted and then beat with egg beater until smooth. Use 2 tbsps. more sugar for this filling. Top with whipped cream, and sprinkle with crushed peppermint stick candy, if desired.

Fruit Filling: (Good for cake, tarts or pie filling) To cream filling add 2 tbsps. drained crushed pineapple, 2 tbsps. drained sliced cherries and a few chopped pecans or filberts.

Currant Tarts

1 cup currants	2 tbsps. melted butter
½ cup corn syrup	1 egg, beaten
½ cup (scant) brown sugar	1 tsp. vanilla

Soften currants in boiling water; drain well and add the other ingredients. Fill tart shells and bake about 20 minutes at 375 degrees.

Coconut Tarts

1 cup sugar	3 egg yolks
2 tbsps. cornstarch	¼ cup butter
½ tsp. salt	1 tsp. vanilla
1 cup water	2 tsps. lemon juice
1 cup (less) shredded coconut	

Mix together in saucepan the sugar, cornstarch and salt. Add water gradually and boil for 1 minute. Stir a little of the hot mixture into the slightly beaten egg yolks, return to saucepan and boil for 1 minute longer, stirring constantly. Remove from heat and add butter, flavoring and coconut. Beat until smooth and pour into cooled baked tart shells. Sprinkle with a little toasted coconut.

Lemon Tarts

¾ cup sugar	1 tbsp. butter
3 tbsps. cornstarch	⅓ cup lemon juice
¼ tsp. salt	Grated rind of 1 orange
¾ cup water	

Mix together in saucepan the first three ingredients; add water gradually and boil, over direct heat, for 1 minute. Remove from heat and stir in the butter. Add lemon juice gradually, and orange rind. Cool slightly and fill tart shells. Top with whipped cream or meringue and sprinkle with a little of the grated orange rind.

Fruit Tarts

Fresh fruit, chopped   2 tbsps. sugar (more or less)
¾ cup fruit juice   1 tbsp. cornstarch

Fill baked tart shells about two-thirds full of chopped fruit. Mix the other ingredients in a saucepan (use sugar according to acidity of fruit), and cook until thick. Pour this over fruit in shells.

Almond Tarts

⅓ lb. almonds, blanched and chopped
2 tbsps. cracker crumbs, rolled and sifted
3 eggs, slightly beaten
1 scant tsp. salt
⅓ cup sugar
2 cups milk
½ tsp. each vanilla and almond extract

Mix together all ingredients. Fill tart shells and bake in oven 375 degrees until firm. Top with a dab of meringue, just before taking from oven.

Puff Paste Roses

Roll out some puff paste about ⅛ inch thick and cut out with a star cutter. Brush over with a little cold water. Fold back the points of the star to the center. Bake, and when nearly done, dust with powdered sugar and return to oven to finish baking. The pastry will puff like a rose. Fill with jelly or a combination of fruit. Serve with a topping of whipped cream or ice cream.

Banana Puffs

Take as many bananas as there are persons to serve. Peel and roll each one in sugar and cinnamon. Roll up in thin pastry and bake in hot oven 450 degrees for about 10 minutes. Serve with whipped cream or Lemon Sauce.

6. Icings, Fillings and Sauces

A cake is more enticing
When covered with icing.
A fowl is more thrilling
With the right kind of filling,
But you know who the boss is
By the use of her sauces.

Quick Strawberry Icing

¾ cup crushed strawberries   ½ cup fine granulated sugar
½ cup confectoner's sugar   1 egg white

Put all together into bowl and beat until consistency to spread.

Clever Judy Icing

1 cup sifted confectioner's   1 tsp. vanilla
    sugar   2 squares unsweetened choco-
1 small egg   late, melted
3 tbsps. milk   1 tbsp. softened butter

Chill bowl in refrigerator. Put all ingredients into chilled bowl and
beat with electric mixer or rotary beater until of spreading consistency. This icing keeps well and does not harden.

Boiled Icing

2 egg whites   2 tsps. lemon juice
1 cup granulated sugar   1 tsp. cream of tartar
3 tbsps. water

Beat over boiling water, in double boiler, until quite stiff. Spread on
cake at once.

Rich Pineapple Icing

½ cup butter
2 egg yolks
⅛ tsp. salt

1 tsp. lemon juice
4 cups sifted icing sugar
Pineapple juice

Cream butter, blend in yolks, salt and lemon juice. Add icing sugar and just enough pineapple juice to make of spreading consistency. A nice icing for an angel cake.

Coffee Foam Icing

1 egg white
1 cup lightly packed brown
    sugar
1 tsp. powdered instant coffee

¼ cup cold water
Few grains salt

Put all ingredients into double boiler and mix thoroughly. Cook over rapidly boiling water until frosting will stand in peaks — about 7 minutes. Remove from heat and blend in ¼ tsp. baking powder and ½ tsp. vanilla. Spread on top and sides of cake. Sufficient for an 8-inch square layer cake.

Fluffy Chocolate Icing

¼ cup soft butter
½ tsp. vanilla
¼ cup sifted confectioner's
    sugar
¼ cup cocoa

1 unbeaten egg white
1¾ cups icing sugar
2 tbsps. boiling water

Cream butter with beater; add vanilla, the ¼ cup icing sugar, and beat well. Add egg white and beat well, then the remaining sugar, and lastly, the boiling water. Beat to spreading consistency.

Plain Butter Icing

Blend together 1½ cups confectioner's sugar and ¼ cup soft butter. Add 2 tbsps. cream or hot water, and flavoring to taste. Cream until mixture is fluffy and stiff enough to spread, adding more sugar, if necessary. This icing may be varied in the following ways:

Orange Icing: Omit cream or water in basic recipe and add orange juice and a little grated rind.

Pineapple Icing: Omit liquid in basic recipe. Add some drained crushed pineapple and enough pineapple juice to mix to right consistency.

Strawberry Icing: Add crushed fresh berries to basic recipe.

Mocha Icing: Add instant powdered coffee to basic recipe, or, omit cream and flavoring in basic recipe and mix with cold coffee infusion.

Chocolate Icing: Add 2 squares unsweetened melted chocolate to basic recipe and a little cream or hot water, if needed.

Jelly and Cheese Icing

Add 4 tbsps. cranberry or any tart jelly to a package of creamed cheese. Gradually fold in a pound of icing sugar. This is sufficient for a 9-inch layer cake.

Apple Snow Icing

Beat white of 1 egg stiff; gradually beat in ¾ cup fine granulated sugar. Grate pulp of 1 apple, a little at a time, and add each portion immediately. Add a little lemon juice and beat with rotary egg beater until quite stiff. Spread on cake and set in cool place.

Note: This icing should be used the same day it is made. A few drops of yellow food coloring and some finely chopped cherries make it quite colorful.

Quick Icing

Combine in top of double boiler ½ cup tart jelly, ¼ tsp. salt, and 1 unbeaten egg white. Place over rapidly boiling water and beat with electric mixer until jelly is free from lumps. Remove from heat and continue beating until icing is stiff enough to spread on cake.

Brown Sugar Glaze

1 cup (packed) brown sugar, 2 tbsps. butter, ¼ cup light cream. Blend ingredients in saucepan and boil over medium heat for 1 minute. Spread on cake while hot.

Ginger Meringue Topping

Beat the whites of 2 eggs until stiff. Add ⅛ tsp. salt and 1 cup brown sugar gradually and beat well. Fold in ⅓ cup chopped, candied or preserved ginger, and spread on cake. Put into oven to brown lightly.

Lemon Filling

1 egg	1 cup sugar
½ cup lemon juice	2½ tbsps. flour
2 tbsps. grated lemon rind	1 tsp. butter

Beat egg until foamy and beat in lemon juice and rind. Combine sugar and flour and beat into egg mixture. Melt butter in a saucepan, remove from heat and add egg mixture. Bring slowly to boiling point over direct heat, stirring constantly. Cover and cool, with occasional stirring, and spread between cake layers.

Lemon-Coconut Filling

½ cup finely cut coconut	1 cup sugar
¼ cup milk	Grated rind and juice of 1 lemon
1 egg	

Combine coconut and milk. Beat egg well. Put all ingredients into double boiler and cook, stirring constantly, until it thickens. Cool and spread between cake layers.

Date Filling

½ lb. chopped dates	2 tbsps. orange juice
½ cup cold water	Grated rind of ½ orange
2 tbsps. brown sugar	1 tsp. lemon juice

Cook dates, water, orange rind and sugar in saucepan, over moderate heat, until thick and smooth. Remove from fire and add fruit juices; stir well and cool before spreading.

Powdered Milk Whipped Cream

½ cup powdered milk	1 tbsp. lemon juice
¼ tsp. vanilla or lemon extract	½ cup cold water
3 tbsps. sugar	

Put water and lemon juice into chilled bowl. Add powdered milk. Stir in sugar and flavoring. Beat until very stiff. Makes about 2½ cups. Best when made just before serving.

Coffee Whipped Cream Filling

Boil together ¾ cup sugar and 1 cup coffee infusion until volume is reduced to about ½ cup. Cool thoroughly and add this syrup slowly to 1 cup of whipped cream.

Fig Filling

¾ lb. figs
¾ cup sugar
½ cup boiling water

Chop figs fine; add sugar and water. Cook to a smooth paste, stirring occasionally. If too stiff, add more water. Spread between cake layers, when cool.

White Sauce

Thin White Sauce: 1 tbsp. butter, 1 tbsp. flour or less, ¼ tsp. salt, ⅛ tsp. pepper, 1 cup milk.

Medium White Sauce: 2 tbsps. butter, 2 tbsps. flour, ¼ tsp. salt, ⅛ tsp. pepper, 1 cup milk.

Thick White Sauce: ¼ cup butter, ¼ cup flour, ¼ tsp. salt, ⅛ tsp. pepper, 1 cup milk.

Melt butter in heavy saucepan, over low heat. Blend in seasonings; cook over low heat until mixture is smooth. Remove from heat and stir in milk. Bring to a boil and cook for 1 minute, stirring constantly.

Horseradish Sauce

Medium White Sauce and add 1 tbsp. or less of prepared horseradish and 1 tsp. prepared mustard, or use the prepared horseradish mustard. Good with beef or any other meat.

Mushroom Sauce

Follow recipe for Medium White Sauce but saute about ¾ cup of sliced mushrooms and a little grated onion in butter, before adding the flour.

Hot Tartar Sauce

To Medium White Sauce add ½ cup mayonnaise, 1 tbsp. grated onion, some minced dill or sweet pickle, parsley and pimiento. This is a good sauce for broccoli.

Curry Sauce

Saute ½ tsp. curry powder in 2 tbsps. butter. Put into top part of double boiler; blend in 2 tbsps. flour, ¼ tsp. salt and ⅛ tsp. pepper. Cook, stirring until mixture is smooth. Add gradually 1 cup milk and cook for about 1 minute longer, stirring constantly. Good with chicken, turkey, duck, or egg dishes.

Cheese Sauce

To 1 cup of Medium White Sauce add 1 cup grated cheese; stir until melted. Use with rice, macaroni, vegetable or egg dishes.

Onion Sauce

Cook 1 cup chopped or sliced onion until soft. Drain and rub through a sieve. Add this to 1 cup Medium White Sauce. Serve with cabbage or any other vegetable.

Tomato Sauce

Saute 1 tbsp. grated or finely chopped onion 1 tbsp. butter. Add 2 tbsps. flour and blend well. Add 1 cup tomato juice or puree; season with pepper and salt. Cook until thick stirring constantly. Serve with fish or any bland food.

Sauce for Fried Halibut

Melt 4 tbsps. butter. Add 2 chopped medium-sized onions. Add 1½ cups hot water, 1 tsp. sugar, 1 tbsp. vinegar. Thicken with about 3 tbsps. flour. Add sliced hard boiled egg, and season to taste with salt and pepper.

Special Sauce

Put into a glass container 2 glasses of vinegar, ½ glass red wine, 1 crushed garlic head, 2 sliced onions, 5 bay leaves, salt. Keep in refrigerator in air tight container and shake well before using. This gives a wonderful flavor if added to meat when cooking, or if used in place of Worchestershire sauce. Especially good with venison.

Cucumber Sauce

1 cup whipped cream, 2 tbsps. lemon juice, dash of cayenne, ¼ tsp. salt, dash of pepper, ¾ cup drained grated cucumber. Stir the lemon juice gradually into the whipped cream, add seasonings and cucumber. Serve with fish.

Vinagrette Sauce

½ cup olive or salad oil, 3 tbsps. vinegar, 1 tsp. salt, paprika and
pepper to taste. To this add a small amount of finely chopped
cucumber pickle, green pepper, hard boiled egg, onion and parsley.
A good sauce to serve with fish.

Sour Cream Sauce

Mix together 1 cup sour cream, 2 tsps. prepared horseradish, 1 tsp.
fresh lemon juice, pinch of salt and white pepper. Serve cold. A nice
compliment for jacket baked potatoes. Chopped chives or parsley
may be added.

Lemon Sauce

Mix ½ cup sugar, 1 tbsp. cornstarch and ⅛ tsp. salt. Gradually add
1 cup boiling water and cook until thick. Add to 1 slightly beaten
egg yolk and cook about 2 minutes longer. Add 2 tbsps. butter, 2
tbsps. lemon juice and 1 tsp. grated lemon rind. Cool slightly and
fold in the beaten egg white.

Orange Sauce

Mix in saucepan 1 cup sugar, ¼ tsp. salt and 2 tbsps. cornstarch. Stir
in 1 cup orange juice, ¼ cup lemon juice and ¾ cup boiling water.
Boil for 1 minute, stirring constantly. Remove from heat and stir in
1 tbsp. butter, and 1 tsp. each grated orange and lemon rind. Serve
hot.

Butterscotch Sauce

Mix in saucepan ¾ cup sugar, ½ cup corn syrup, ¼ tsp. salt, ¼ cup
butter, ½ cup cream or evaporated milk. Cook over low heat, stirring
to soft ball stage. Stir in an additional ½ cup cream and cook to
thick, smooth consistency. Remove from heat and stir in ½ tsp.
vanilla. Serve hot or cold.

Hot Chocolate Sauce

Melt 2 oz. unsweetened chocolate in a double boiler. Add 1 tbsp.
butter and gradually stir in ⅓ cup boiling water. Stir well and add
1 cup sugar and 2 tbsps. corn syrup. Boil rapidly over direct heat for
5 minutes. When ready to serve add 1 tsp. vanilla. An excellent sauce
for ice cream.

Fluffy Chocolate Sauce

Put into top part of double boiler 2 squares unsweetened chocolate, 1 cup sugar, 1 large tin evaporated milk, ¼ cup water, ½ cup corn syrup, 2 tsps. vanilla and ¼ tsp. salt. When chocolate is melted, beat with egg beater until blended. Cook for a few minutes until it thickens slightly. This sauce thickens more as it cools.

Soft Custard Sauce

Scald 1½ cups milk in top of double boiler. Beat 2 eggs well, add ¼ cup sugar, ¼ tsp. salt, and gradually stir into this the scalded milk. Return to double boiler and cook slowly, stirring constantly. When custard coats a silver spoon, remove from heat. If custard should curdle, beat at once with egg beater until smooth. Add 1 tsp. vanilla. Use over Snow Pudding and other desserts.

Sunshine Sauce

Whip together until stiff 1 cup whipping cream and ½ cup confectioner's sugar. Blend in 2 well beaten egg yolks and 2 tbsps. brandy or any other flavoring. Use over steamed puddings.

Hard Sauce

Cream until soft ½ cup butter. Gradually blend in 1 cup icing sugar. Beat in 1 unbeaten egg white and ½ tsp vanilla. Chill.

Raisin Sauce

Cook until tender ¾ cup raisins and 1 cup water. Add ¾ cup sugar, 1 tbsp. cornstarch, 1 tbsp. butter, 1 tbsp. vinegar, 1 tsp. lemon juice and about 5 whole cloves. Cook until it thickens. If too thick, add a little hot water. Serve with baked ham.

Toffee Sauce

Combine and stir over low heat 1 cup light cream, 1 cup corn syrup, 1-2 tbsps. butter, ⅛ tsp. salt. Beat with egg beater until well blended and smooth. Add vanilla.

Strawberry Sauce

Cream ⅓ cup butter and 1 cup powdered sugar, adding the sugar gradually. Add ⅔ cup fresh strawberries, a few at a time, beating between additions until well blended. Fold in the stiffly beaten white of 1 egg.

Pleasing Pudding Sauce

Mix well ⅓ cup (packed) brown sugar, 3 tbsps. cornstarch and ¼ tsp. salt. Gradually stir in 1¾ cups boiling water. Cook slowly, stirring constantly, until thickened. Cover and continue cooking until no raw flavor of starch remains. Stir in ⅓ cup corn syrup. Remove from heat and stir in 1½ tbsps. butter, ½ tsp. vanilla and ¼ cup sherry. Heat before serving.

Coffee Sauce

Make a soft custard of 1 cup clear strong coffee, 3 egg yolks (beaten) and ⅓ cup sugar. Delicious with vanilla or coffee ice cream.

Parsley Sauce

Follow recipe for Medium White Sauce and add 1 tsp. lemon juice, a few grains of cayenne. Add about 4 tbsps. finely chopped parsley just before serving. Boiling water may be substituted for the milk. Good with vegetable dishes or fish.

Cranberry Sauce

Cook 3 cups cranberries and 1 cup water until soft. Add 1½ cups sugar and bring just to the boiling point. Let simmer on back of stove for about 30 minutes. This makes a thick sauce but will not jell if allowed to boil after the sugar is added.

Drawn Butter Sauce

Melt 4 tbsps. butter in top part of double boiler. Add slowly 2 tbsps. flour and blend well. Add ½ tsp. salt, ⅛ tsp. pepper and 1 tsp. lemon juice. Slowly add to this 1 cup stock or water. Cook, stirring constantly, until thickened.

Spiced Whipped Cream Sauce

Whip 1 cup cream; add 1 tsp. sugar, ¼ tsp. cinnamon, ½ tsp. vanilla, 2 tbsps. molasses or less, and a little salt. Excellent topping for Apple Dumplings or Cottage Pudding.

Variation: To the whipped cream add ¼ cup powdered sugar, ½ cup raspberry syrup.

Caramel Sauce

In a saucepan over low heat cook together 1¼ cups brown sugar, ⅔ cup light corn syrup, ¼ cup butter, and a pinch of salt until the sugar is dissolved. Continue to cook the mixture until it forms a firm ball when a drop is tested in cold water. Remove the syrup from the heat and stir in ½ cup heavy cream and ½ tsp. vanilla. Let sauce cool before using. Makes about 1½ cups.

7.   Ice Cream and Candy

If you have a party or social affair,
Ice cream and candy are always there.

For making this ice cream in the refrigerator, ice cream powders such as junket or rennet are necessary. Various flavors are obtainable but vanilla flavoring is the most practical as any other flavor may be successfully added to change, completely, the vanilla flavoring.

Vanilla Ice Cream (Basic Recipe)

1 pkg. rennet powder
1 cup milk
1 cup cream, chilled and whipped

Pour milk over ice cream powder and mix until powder is thoroughly dissolved. Fold this slowly into the stiffly beaten cream. Turn quickly into freezing tray and freeze at highest point for 1 hour. Turn back control to keep the ice cream at freezing temperature.

Coffee Ice Cream: In basic recipe, in place of milk, use 1 cup strong black coffee infusion and add 1 level teaspoon powdered instant coffee.

Banana Ice Cream: Add mashed banana and juice of half a lemon to basic recipe.

Pineapple Ice Cream: Add well drained, crushed pineapple (quantity depending on taste) to basic recipe.

Strawberry Ice Cream: Add less milk, allowing for juice of berries, and 1 cup well sweetened, crushed strawberries, to basic recipe.

Burnt Almond Ice Cream: To basic recipe add ⅓ cup finely chopped unblanched toasted almonds. Almonds must be well browned to give true flavor but watched carefully to prevent scorching. Cool thoroughly before adding to cream mixture.

Ginger Ice Cream: Cut up very fine, about three tablespoons preserved ginger root, or candied ginger (the former preferred). Add a little syrup from the bottle of ginger root, and fold this into the basic recipe.

Grapenut Ice Cream: Add ½ cup or more grapenuts to milk and powder in basic recipe.

Mint Ice Cream: To the basic recipe add ¼ tsp. mint flavoring (more, according to taste) and add a few drops of green food coloring. Serve this ice cream with Hot Chocolate Sauce.

Note: Finely crushed peppermint stick candy soaked in the milk for several hours may be substituted for mint flavoring.

Standard Ice Cream

1¼ cup milk
2 eggs
½ cup sugar
1 tbsp. flour

⅛ tsp. salt
1 cup cream or chilled evaporated
    milk
2 tsps. vanilla

Scald milk. Beat egg yolks; add sugar and flour. Combine with hot milk and cook over low heat until mixture coats a spoon, like a thin custard. Cool. Beat egg whites until stiff; add salt and fold into custard. Add vanilla. Pour into tray and put into freezing unit to freeze to a mush. Remove from freezing tray and beat until smooth. Fold in whipped cream or whipped milk and freeze for 2 to 3 hours.

Note: This ice cream may be varied in the same way as preceding recipe. Always use less milk if using cold coffee infusion or fruit juice, keeping liquid to 1¼ cups. If fruit is added, fold into mixture when adding whipped cream.

Lemon Cream Sherbet

1 pint milk, very cold
2 lemons, juice and a little
    grated rind

1½ cups sugar
3 eggs, beaten
2 cups cream, whipped

Mix together lemon juice and sugar; add to milk slowly, stirring constantly. These directions, if followed exactly, should prevent curdling of milk. Add beaten eggs, and lastly fold in whipped cream. Stir occasionally while freezing. Freeze like ice cream.

Orange Sherbet

2 tsps. gelatin
¼ cup cold water
1 cup water
¾ cup sugar (less)
1 tsp. grated lemon rind

1 tsp. grated orange rind
1½ cups orange juice
⅓ cup lemon juice
⅛ tsp. salt
2 stiffly beaten egg whites

Soak gelatin in ¼ cup cold water. Boil the 1 cup water and sugar for 10 minutes. Put the gelatin into the hot syrup and cool. Add the grated rind and juices. Fold into this chilled mixture the stiffly beaten egg whites and salt. Freeze as for lemon sherbet.

Strawberry or Raspberry Sherbet

2 heaping cups fresh hulled
    berries
1 cup sugar
½ pint thick sour cream
¾ cup milk

1½ cups sugar
1 well beaten egg
¼ cup lemon juice

Crush berries; add 1 cup sugar and let stand for 30 minutes. Combine sour cream, milk and the 1½ cups sugar; stir until sugar is dissolved. Add egg, lemon juice and berries; mix well. Pour into freezer tray and freeze until firm but not solid. Break into chunks and beat with electric mixer until smooth but not melted. Freeze as for ice cream.

Orange and Lemon Cream

Juice of 1 orange
Juice of 1 lemon
Grated rind of ½ orange
Grated rind of ½ lemon

½ cup sugar
⅛ tsp. salt
½ pint cream, whipped

Mix the juices, rind sugar and salt and let stand until sugar is dissolved, stirring occasionally. Add the whipped cream and freeze at coldest point for 1 hour or longer. This is nice served with Sponge Cake or Whipped Cream Cake.

Cocoa Fudge

2 cups white sugar
6 tbsps. cocoa
¾ cup milk

Stir over quick heat until the sugar is dissolved. Cook very, very slowly to the soft ball stage 238 degrees, stirring only if necessary. Remove from fire and add, without stirring, 2 tbsps. butter. Cool, and when nearly cold add 1 tsp. vanilla. Beat until it is creamy and just before pouring into buttered pan add 1 cup of nut meats or raisins. Cut in squares before it hardens. If desired, Rice Krispies or any crisp cereal may be used instead of the nuts and raisins.

Chocolate Fudge

Boil for 5 minutes, stirring constantly. Remove from stove.

5 cups white sugar
1 large can evaporated milk

¼ cup butter
¼ tsp. salt

Add:

1 tbsp. vanilla
2 cups nut meats
1 large jar marshmallow

2 pkgs. semi-sweet chocolate bits
½ lb. pkg. sweet chocolate

Stir until all the chocolate is melted. Pour into a very large pan (15 × 9) and cut in squares when cool. Store in tins and keep in refrigerator. This fudge never gets hard. Recipe may be halved.

Chocolate Marshmallow Fudge

2 squares unsweetened
        chocolate, cut in pieces
⅔ cup cold milk
2 cups sugar

2 tbsps. butter
1 tsp. vanilla
¼ tsp. salt

Add chocolate to milk and cook over low flame until mixture is smooth, stirring constantly. Add sugar and salt and stir until sugar is dissolved and mixture boils. Continue cooking, without stirring, until a small amount of mixture forms a very soft ball in cold water. Remove from fire. Add butter and vanilla. When cooled to lukewarm beat until it thickens and begins to lose its gloss. Pour very quickly over marshmallows which have been cut in halves and placed cut side up in buttered pan, 8 × 4 inches. When cold, cut in squares.

Peanut Butter Fudge

2 cups white sugar
2 cups light brown sugar

¾ cups milk
½ tsp. salt

Mix above in large saucepan and bring to a boil. Boil 5 minutes only. Remove from stove and add: 1 18-oz jar peanut butter, 1 7½ oz jar of marshmallow cream, 1 cup chopped nuts (optional), and 1 tsp. vanilla. Mix quickly as this soon hardens. Turn into 2 well buttered 8 × 8″ pans. As soon as set, cut into squares.

Jello Divinity Fudge

3 cups white sugar   2 egg whites
¾ cup corn syrup   3½ tbsps. jello
¾ cup water

Cook first three ingredients until mixture forms a hard ball when tested in cold water. Beat egg whites stiff. Add jello powder gradually. Add syrup in steady stream; beat until it loses its gloss and pour into buttered pan. Cut in squares when cold.

Ginger Candy

2 cups white sugar   ¾ cup milk
1 cup brown sugar   2 tbsps. corn syrup

Cook above ingredients slowly to the soft ball stage 238 degrees, stirring often. Remove from fire, add 2 tbsps. butter and let cool. Beat until it begins to thicken and add 1 tsp. vanilla and ¼ lb. finely Chopped ginger. If candied ginger is used, wash and dry thoroughly to remove sugar. Pour candy into buttered pan and cut in squares before it hardens.

Vinegar Candy

2 cups white sugar
½ cup vinegar
2 tbsps. butter

Put butter into saucepan and when melted add sugar and vinegar. Stir until sugar is dissolved, afterwards stirring occasionally. Boil, until when tried in cold water, mixture will become brittle. Pour on buttered platter to cool. Pull and cut as for molasses candy.

Coconut Drops

1 cup white sugar   ½ cup coconut
1 cup brown sugar   2 tsps. butter
½ cup milk   ½ tsp. vanilla

Cook sugar and milk until it forms a soft ball when tested in cold water. Add remaining ingredients and beat until it begins to show signs of thickening. Drop quickly, like cookies, on buttered wax paper. Do not over beat.

Jiffy Crispies

¼ cup butter
½ cup marshmallows
5 cups rice krispies

Melt butter, add marshmallows and cook over low heat, stirring constantly, until marshmallows are melted. Remove from heat. Add rice krispies and stir until well coated with marshmallow mixture. Press into a buttered 13 × 9 inch pan. When cool, cut in squares.

Peanut Crisp

2 cups white sugar
1 cup peanuts
½ tsp. salt

Melt sugar slowly in heavy pan. Put peanuts, previously crisped, into buttered pan and sprinkle with salt. Pour the melted sugar over peanuts. When cold, break in pieces.

Party Pick-ups

1½ cups butter, melted
9 cups Cheerios
4 cups Shreddies
4 cups Pretzels, cut in small
   pieces
2½ cups salted peanuts

Put all ingredients into large roaster and stir well with wooden spoon. Add 1 tbsp. garlic salt, 1 tbsp. celery salt and 2½ tbsps. Worcestershire sauce. Bake slowly in oven 250 degrees for 1½ hours or longer. Stir several times. Keep in air tight containers.

Mock Strawberries

Mix together:

1 can condensed milk
2 pkgs. strawberry jello

Mix and add to above mixture ¾ to 1 lb. dessicated coconut, 1 tbsp. white sugar, ½ tsp. red food coloring. Let stand in refrigerator over night. Shape to form strawberries. Roll in ½ pkg. of strawberry jello (undissolved crystals). Press dent in top to resemble strawberry. Top with leaf and stem made of green icing. Let set over night for best results. These are tasty and attractive.

8. Pickles and Preserves

Cucumbers, celery onions and beets
Are a treat made into these pickled receipts.

Bread and Butter Pickles

6 large onions
6 qts. sliced unpared
   cucumbers
1 cup salt
1 qt. cider vinegar

6 cups sugar
⅓ cup mustard seed
1½ tbsps. celery seed
¼ tsp. cayenne

Slice onions and combine with cucumbers and salt; let stand 3 hours and drain well. Combine vinegar, sugar, mustard and celery seed, cayenne; bring to boiling point and let boil for 5 minutes. Add cucumbers and onions. Heat to simmering point but do not permit pickles to boil. Place the pickles in hot sterilized jars and seal at once.

Note: Green or red peppers and tumeric may be added, if desired.

Mustard Pickles

4 qts. cucumbers, cut in small
   pieces
2 qts. small onions

1 cauliflower, separated in small
   flowerets
3 red and 1 green peppers,
   chopped fine

Soak cucumbers overnight with ½ cup salt and water to cover. Drain well. Put into large pot and cover with dressing made as follows:

Put on stove 1 quart vinegar and 5 cups sugar and let come to a boil. With another quart vinegar mix the following ingredients to a smooth paste: 1½ cups flour, 12 tbsps. dry mustard, 2 tbsps. tumeric, 1 tsp. curry (optional). Combine with heated vinegar and sugar and add to vegetables. Let stand on back of stove for several hours, stirring occasionally, but do not boil. Seal while hot.

Dutch Salad

2 qts. cucumbers, cut in small   2 qts. green tomatoes, chopped
    pieces   1 small cabbage, cut fine
2 qts. onions, chopped

Cover above ingredients with 1 cup salt; add boiling water to cover and let stand for 1 hour. Drain well.

Make a dressing with 7 cups vinegar, 6 cups sugar, 3 tbsps. mustard, 2 cups flour, 2 tsps. tumeric. Cook until thick and smooth. Add vegetables and simmer until heated through. Do not boil. Put into air tight bottles and seal while hot.

Special Day Pickles

Select cucumbers about 6 inches long. Soak in ice water 5 hours or longer. Cut in lengthwise pieces, without paring, and pack closely in jars with about three pieces of celery and 3 or 4 slices of onion. Drain off any juice after bottles have been packed.

Put on stove 1 quart vinegar, 1 cup sugar, ½ cup water, ⅓ cup salt and boil this well. Pour it over the pickles, filling bottles, and seal at once. Allow about 4 weeks for this pickle to mellow before using.

Pickled Green Beans

12 cups cut beans
1 cup fine salt
1 cup white sugar

Mix together and press overnight. In the morning fill air tight bottles, adding the brine. Seal. Soak beans before cooking.

Cucumber Relish

Put through food chopper and sprinkle with ¼ cup salt. Let stand overnight.

7 large cucumbers
5 medium-sized onions

Drain very well. Make a dressing of the following:

1½ cups brown sugar, ½ cup flour, 1 tsp. tumeric, 1 cup sugar, 3 tsps. dry mustard, 1 tsp. ginger, 3 cups vinegar, 1 cup water. Mix dry ingredients with a little of the vinegar. Bring the remaining vinegar and water to a boil. Mix the paste with a little of the heated vinegar and combine; cook until thick. Add cucumber mixture and cook slowly for about 15 minutes. Seal while hot.

Cranberry and Apple Relish

4 cups cranberries, uncooked   1 lemon
2 apples, pared and cored   2½ cups sugar
2 oranges

Put fruit through food chopper. Add sugar and mix well. Chill for several hours. This will keep for several weeks, if kept in refrigerator.

Cranberry Relish

1 qt. cranberries, uncooked   2 cups sugar
2 oranges, rind and pulp   ½ cup crushed pineapple

Put cranberries and oranges through food chopper. Add sugar and pineapple; stir until well combined. Keep in refrigerator.

Beet Relish

4 cups chopped cooked beets   ¼ tsp. pepper
4 cups chopped cabbage   2 cups vinegar
¼ cup or more horseradish   1 cup sugar
     mustard
2 tsps. salt

Combine the beets, cabbage and horseradish mustard; add salt and pepper. Bring vinegar to the boiling point, add sugar and when dissolved add to first mixture. Cook until vegetables are tender. Seal while hot in tight sterilized jars.

Cranberry Catchup

1 lb. onions   1 tbsp. ground cloves
4 lbs. cranberries   1 tbsp. cinnamon
2 cups water   1 tbsp. allspice
4 cups sugar   1 tbsp. salt
2 cups vinegar   1 tsp. pepper

Peel onions and chop very fine. Add cranberries and water; cook until tender. Put through a sieve. Add remaining ingredients and boil until thick, stirring occasionally. Pour into hot sterilized bottles and seal. Serve with meat or fowl.

Tomato Catchup

1 peck ripe tomatoes	1 tbsp. mixed pickling spice
6 onions, sliced	1 tbsp. celery seed
1 small garlic clove	1 tsp. cayenne
2 red peppers, seeded	½ cup sugar
2 small bay leaves	2 cups vinegar
1 tbsp. salt	12 black peppercorns

Boil first six ingredients until soft. Put through sieve. Tie spices in a cheesecloth bag and add, with the sugar, to tomato pulp. Boil rapidly, stirring occasionally, until thick. Remove spices, add vinegar and boil for ten minutes longer. Seal, at once, in hot sterilized bottles.

Winter Salad

8 green tomatoes	1 bunch celery
6 large onions	2 sweet red peppers
1 small head cabbage	

Chop above ingredients. Put into pot and pour vinegar over to come within 1 inch of top. Boil 15 minutes. Add 3 lbs. sugar, 2 tbsps. salt, 1 tsp. tumeric, 2 tbsps. mustard, 1 cup flour. Boil a few minutes longer and bottle.

Chow-Chow

1 peck green tomatoes
10 large onions

Slice tomatoes and sprinkle each layer with salt, using about ½ cup. Let stand overnight. Drain thoroughly. Place layers of tomatoes and sliced onions in a large pot. Add 1 quart vinegar, 1 cup sugar and 4 tbsps. whole pickling spice tied in a piece of cheesecloth. Simmer slowly for about four hours, adding 3 more cups sugar, at intervals. Stir often to prevent scorching.

Note: To make Mustard Chow add about 2 tbsps. dry mustard and ½ tsp. tumeric.

Dill Pickles

Select and wash small to medium sized cucumbers and pack in sterilized jars with 2 or 3 heads of fresh dill. A clove of garlic improves the flavor and may be added, if desired. Make a brine of 3 qts.

water, 1 qt. cider vinegar and 1 cup coarse salt. Bring this to a boil and pour over cucumbers while boiling hot. Seal at once. Sufficient to make 5 to 6 qts. pickles, closely packed.

Lazy Housewife Pickles

1 gallon cider vinegar	1 cup salt
1 cup dry mustard	2 or 3 cups brown sugar

Mix until smooth, sugar, mustard and salt with a little of the vinegar. Add remaining vinegar. Put this into a large crock, and add small whole unpared cucumbers, or large ones cut in long pieces. A small bag of whole pickling spice may be added. Pickles are ready for use after several days. More cucumbers may be added when picked from the garden. Cover the crock with a plate and keep a weight on it. These will keep for a year and will always be brittle.

Celery Sauce

6 bunches celery	1 peck ripe tomatoes
8 or 10 large onions	4 sweet red peppers, seeds
1⅓ cups brown sugar	removed
4 cups vinegar	⅓ cup salt

Chop vegetables. Combine with other ingredients and boil for 2 hours. Bottle while hot.

Spiced Currants

3½ lbs. currants	½ tsp. salt
2½ lbs. brown sugar	1 tbsp. cinnamon
½ pint vinegar	¼ tsp. nutmeg
¼ tsp. allspice	1 tsp. cloves

Wash, drain and remove stems from currants. Put into pot with other ingredients; bring to boiling point and cook slowly for 1½ hours. Seal in sterilized jars.

Sweet Pickled Peaches

7 lbs. peaches	1-oz. stick cinnamon
3½ lbs. brown sugar	Cloves to taste
1 pint vinegar	

Boil for 20 minutes, sugar, vinegar, cinnamon, and cloves. Dip peaches quickly in hot water and rub off the peeling. Put into the hot syrup and cook until soft but not too well done. Do one-half the peaches at a time. Place in sterilized jars and pour the hot syrup over fruit. Seal air tight.

Ripe Tomato Marmalade

1 quart ripe tomatoes	2 oranges
2 lbs. sugar	2 lemons

Cut tomatoes, bring to a boil, and remove the skin. Remove pulp from oranges and lemons. Boil rind until tender. Cut in small strips with scissors. Put all together and boil slowly for about 2 hours, stirring occasionally. Bottle while hot.

Rose Hip Puree

Gather rose hips while red (wild rose or ordinary garden rose seed pods may be used). Chill. Remove blossom ends and stems. Wash quickly. To 1½ cups boiling water add 1 cup rose hips. Cover cooking utensil and simmer for 15 minutes. Crush and let stand in a pottery container for 24 hours. Drain off extract and bring it to a rolling boil. Add 2 tsps. lemon juice for every pint of liquid. Pour into sterile jars and seal. (Never use copper of aluminum utensils for cooking rose hips).

Note: Two tablespoonfuls of this extract should supply the daily dose of Vitamin C.

Strawberry Preserves

Put 4 cups hulled washed berries into heavy pan, including some under ripe ones. Add 1 tbsp. vinegar; bring to boil, cover and boil for 1 minute. Add 3 cups sugar; bring to boil. Boil gently, uncovered, for 20 minutes. Stir occasionally to keep laggards from sticking to bottom. Pour hot berries into bowl and let stand overnight. Fruit will look very liquid but plumps up and absorbs syrup as it stands. Next morning ladle cold fruit into sterilized jars; cover immediately with ⅛ inch of melted paraffin. Recipe makes 5 or 6 (5½ oz.) glasses.

Green Tomato Mincemeat

7 lbs. green tomatoes
8 medium sized apples, unpeeled

Put tomatoes and apples through food grinder and add the following ingredients:

3 lbs. brown sugar	¼ tbsp. salt
1 lb. raisins	¼ cup cider vinegar
1½ tsps. cinnamon	½ lb. margarine
1 tbsp. ground cloves	1½ lbs. ground meat
1 tbsp. allspice or ground nutmeg	1 cup mixed peel
	1 cup crushed pineapple

Spices may be added, as preferred. Let simmer slowly for about two hours. Bottle while hot.

Delicious Meatless Mince Meat

2 lbs. currants	3 tbsps. salt
2½ lbs. brown sugar	1 tsp. cloves
2 lbs. raisins	2 tsps. nutmeg
2 or more large tart apples	1 pkg. cherries, cut
2 cups ground suet	½ lb. citron peel
2 lemons	¼ lb. candied orange peel
2 tsps. ginger	

Squeeze juice from lemons. Boil rinds, starting them in cold water. When soft put through food chopper, using fine knife. Mix fruits together. Add other ingredients. Simmer for 1 hour or longer. This keep indefinitely. Good for pies and tarts.

Preserved Citron

Peel citron and remove seeds; cut in inch squares. Measure 1 pound of sugar for each pound of citron used. Make a syrup of the sugar and water and boil for 20 minutes. Add the citron and cook slowly until tender and transparent. When done add 2 thinly sliced lemons. Let stand about 10 minutes. Bottle while hot.

Cranberry Jelly

Cook 1 quart of cranberries with ½ cup water until berries burst. Mash the pulp through a sieve; add 2 cups sugar and cook until smooth. Pour into a pan to cool. This jelly, diced or cut with fancy cutters, is nice to garnish a chicken or turkey platter.

Rhubarb Jam

5 cups rhubarb, cut small   1 20-oz. can crushed pineapple
5 cups sugar   2 pkgs. strawberry jello

Combine first three ingredients and let stand overnight. Boil for 20 minutes. Remove from stove and add jello. Stir until well dissolved and put in airtight jars.

9.   Beverages

Rhubarb Juice

Cut rhubarb and stew in water; strain through cheesecloth.

2½ lbs. rhubarb
2 qts. water

Add:

1¼ cups sugar
Juice of 2 lemons

Juice of 1 orange
4 whole cloves

Keep in refrigerator. This is ready for use when cold. Delicious.

Fruit Juice

Heat this but do not boil. Cool.

1 can apple juice
1 cup sugar

Add:

1 can apple juice
1 can pineapple juice

Juice of 3 oranges
Juice of 1 lemon

Keep in refrigerator and when ready to serve add 1 quart bottle gingerale.

Ginger Punch

1 qt. water
1 cup sugar
½ cup pineapple juice

½ cup lemon juice
½ cup orange juice
½ cup (less) chopped preserved
ginger

Boil water, ginger and sugar slowly for 15 minutes. Add fruit juices and chill. Dilute with ice water.

Shirriff's Punch
(My prize winning recipe)

1 jar SHIRRIFF'S Red
   Currant Jelly
Juice of 4 oranges and 3
   lemons

½ cup sugar
1 large bottle ginger ale

Beat jelly with egg beater until quite frothy. Add 2 cups boiling water, fruit juices and sugar. Chill and just before serving add ginger ale.

Iced Tea

4 cups strong hot tea
Juice of 3 lemons

1 cup (less) sugar
A few sprigs of bruised mint

Chill above ingredients. Strain and when ready to serve add 2 cups ginger ale. Serve in tall glasses and garnish with lemon or orange wedges, mint sprigs.

Iced Coffee

Prepare strong coffee. Pour in refrigerator cube tray and freeze. Put several cubes into glass and pour over cubes freshly made hot weak coffee. Cream and sugar to taste. Nice topped with ice cream.

Hot Chocolate

½ cup cream
2 heaping tbsps. cocoa

1 egg
¼ cup sugar

Whip cream. Add cocoa, egg and sugar; beat until stiff. Use about 1 teaspoon to 1 cup hot milk.

Russian Tea

Juice of 4 oranges
Juice of 1 lemon
Grated rind of ½ orange
Grated rind of ½ lemon

1¼ cups sugar
8 cups water
8 whole cloves

Bring above ingredients to boiling point and pour it over 5 level teaspoons of tea. Cover and let stand for 5 minutes. Strain and cool. This will keep for an indefinite time in refrigerator. Reheat, but do not boil. May also be served cold. Pineapple juice may be added, if desired.

Raspberry Vinegar

Fill a jar with ripe raspberries. Press lightly and add as much vinegar as the jar will hold or use 1 pint of vinegar to 2 quarts of berries. Let stand for two weeks and strain. Add 1 pound of white sugar to every pint of juice used. Boil 20 minutes. While hot put into sterile air tight bottles. Dilute with water.

Note: Currants may be used in the same way.

Energy Drink

Beat 2 eggs well. Add juice of an orange and a little sugar.

Party Ice Cubes

Fill sectioned ice cube tray with any preferred juice or drink. Into each section put either a maraschino cherry, lemon cube, orange cube, or a mint leaf. Freeze.

Beverage Syrups

Syrup for Milk Shakes: 4 squares unsweetened chocolate melted or 1 cup cocoa, $\frac{1}{8}$ tsp. salt, 1 cup sugar, 2 cups water. Boil for about 5 minutes. Keep in covered container in refrigerator. Add a little vanilla flavoring, if desired, when mixing drink.

Hot Maple Syrup: Combine 1 cup corn syrup, $\frac{1}{2}$ cup brown sugar and $\frac{1}{3}$ cup water. Cook, stirring until sugar is dissolved. Add a few drops of maple flavoring and 1 tablespoon butter. Serve hot.

Simple Syrup: Mix 2 cups sugar and 1 cup water. Bring to a boil and boil for 5 minutes without stirring. When cool, bottle and keep in cool place. This syrup saves time, blends better, and is excellent for fruit drinks, milk shakes and for many other uses.

Amber Syrup: Put 2 cups molasses and 4 tbsps. butter into a saucepan. Bring to a full boil, take from stove and add 3 tbsps. cider vinegar. Mix well and cool.

Index

Printed in Canada